Sense

The Diaries

Sense
&
Sensibility

The Diaries

EMMA THOMPSON
with photographs by Clive Coote

BLOOMSBURY

ACKNOWLEDGEMENTS
I should like to acknowledge the profoundest debt
(for my having developed any sense of humour)
to Jane Austen, Monty Python
and the Magic Roundabout

First published in Great Britain 1995
This paperback edition published 1996

Bloomsbury Publishing Plc, 38 Soho Square, London W1V 5DF

A CIP catalogue record for this book is available from the British Library

10 9 8 7 6 5 4 3 2 1

ISBN 0 7475 3060 2

Typeset by Hewer Text Composition Services, Edinburgh
Printed by St Edmundsbury Press, Bury St Edmunds

The Diaries

Preamble

Production meeting in Oxford Street on a raw wintry morning on Monday 15 January 1995. Lindsay Doran (producer), James Schamus (co-producer), Ang Lee (director) and I had met previously this month to discuss the latest draft of the script, which is what we're all here to work through. Tony Clarkson (locations manager) and Laurie Borg (co-producer) already know one another but this is the first time the core personnel of the shoot have met to prepare.

Lindsay goes round the table and introduces everyone – making it clear that I am present in the capacity of writer rather than actress, therefore no one has to be too nice to me. It's 9 a.m. and everyone looks a bit done in. Except Ang, who brings self-contained calm wherever he goes. Just looking at him makes me feel frazzled in comparison, as though all my hair's standing on end.

Our first point of discussion is the hunt (during which, in this version, we witness the accident that kills Mr Dashwood). Where do we get a hunt? It seems to require at least twenty-five male stunt riders – or we hire a real hunt, like the Beaufort which was used on *The Remains of the Day*. Ang wants villagers and labourers watching and to see the fox being chased. My idea is to start the film with an image of the vixen locked out of her lair which has been plugged up. Her terror as she's pursued across the country. This is a big deal. It means training a fox from birth or dressing up a dog to look like a fox. Or hiring David Attenborough, who probably knows a few foxes well enough to ask a favour. Laurie finally says it's impossible.

What Ang wants next is even more expensive: he's desperate for a kitchen scene in Norland Park (home to the Dashwoods – to be filmed at Saltram House in Devon) which would show the entire staff of Norland preparing a huge meal. I want a bleeding Mr Dashwood to be brought in through the kitchen door and laid on the table surrounded by all the raw joints of meat. As Ang and I enthuse about symbolism, Laurie gently reminds us of expense. These are costly scenes and the film hasn't even started.

I look around the table and realise – perhaps for the first time – that it's actually going to happen. After five years' work on the script (albeit intermittent), the sense of released energy is palpable. There are budgets, an office and several real people here. I glaze over for a second, in shock. Pulled out of reverie by James asking, yet again, what physical activities can be found for Elinor and Marianne. Painting, sewing, embroidering, writing letters, pressing leaves, it's all depressingly girlie. Chin-ups, I suggest, but promise to think further.

We start to work through the entire script, adding, subtracting, bargaining, negotiating, trying to save money wherever we can. We get to the ballroom sequence and I suggest that we create several vignettes that occur in the background – a rich old rake forcing his attentions on a young girl whose greedy father affects not to notice, a fat matriarch surrounded by sycophantic cousins – a Cruikshankian taste of nine-teenth-century greed and hypocrisy. More expensive than simply filling the room with extras but much more interesting. Laurie's eyes roll but he agrees that it's worth the effort and money.

I have a notion that it might be nice to see Colonel Brandon tickling trout – something to draw Marianne to him. Tickling trout is a mysterious old country method of catching trout; you tickle their tummies and when they're relaxed you whip them out of the water. I ask Laurie if it's possible to get trained fish. Lindsay says this is how we know I've never produced a movie. She tells us that two of her friends had read the script and thought I'd invented the pregnancy of Brandon's family ward for shock value. It's surprising to find such events in Austen, but after all, how many people know that there's a duel in *Sense and Sensibility*? When Lindsay asked me to adapt the novel I thought that *Emma* or *Persuasion* would have been better. In fact there's more action in *S & S* than I'd remembered and its elements translate to drama very effectively.

We get to the end of the script by 3.20 p.m. and Lindsay says, 'Can we afford the movie we just described?' It's a long, complex script and the budget is pushed to the limit. James is most worried about the number of shooting days. Doesn't seem enough. (In the event, our fifty-eight days stretched to sixty-five.)

Wander out into Oxford Street slightly dazed. 'See you in April,' I say to Laurie. Now everyone goes their separate ways to continue prep. Ang and James return to New York and work on budget and schedule from there. Lindsay returns to LA to produce and I go to West Hampstead and switch the computer on. Another draft . . .

I spend the rest of January in tears and a black dressing gown.

During February and March I revise the script constantly but the basic structure remains the same. Half a dozen new drafts hit the presses but by 2 April we settle on the final shooting draft. The hunt and kitchen scenes discussed at the January production meeting have both been cut due to budget and schedule constraints.

In February, Ang, James and Lindsay return and the casting process begins. We start with Fanny. Everyone we see captures perfectly the balance of wifely concern and vicious self-interest. Ang says at the end of one day, 'This is a nation of Fannys.' It rings horribly true. Some characters are far more elusive, notably Lucy Steele and Willoughby, perhaps because of their hidden motives. Gemma Jones, Kate Winslet and Elizabeth Spriggs are so immediately Mrs Dashwood, Marianne and Mrs Jennings that we find it difficult to imagine anyone else in the roles. I'm excited about the fact that five of the actors I prevailed upon to perform a reading of an early draft last year are all hired by Ang: Hugh Grant (Edward), Robert Hardy (Sir John), Harriet Walter (Fanny), Imelda Staunton (Charlotte Palmer) and Hugh Laurie (Mr Palmer). Also that Hugh Grant, for whom I wrote Edward, has agreed to do it despite having become after *Four Weddings* the most famous man in the world. It's odd to be on the other side of the casting process. Even though Michelle Guish, the casting director, makes the circumstances as relaxed as possible, I am uncomfortably aware of how difficult it is for an actor to walk into a small room full of people staring at them. Lindsay is quite shy, James chats a bit, Ang seldom says anything at all and I make a lot of irrelevant noise whenever there's a long silence. Ang's principal criteria are unexpected. Physiognomy matters a great deal to him. Not whether a person is good-looking but the spaces between their lower lip and chin and between the bridge of the nose and forehead. Praxitelean proportions, virtually. After a first meeting with an actor there's a second during which we read scenes. I get the opportunity to play all the other roles and have a minor success with Sir John. Then a third when the scenes are put on video. Ang is not familiar with many British actors so we see people time and again until he's certain of what he wants.

'Can everyone in England act?' he says after a particularly engaging afternoon. Lindsay and I think about this one for quite some time before deciding that probably the answer is yes.

Ang presents a collection of intriguing contradictions. He does t'ai chi but his shoulders are constantly bowed, he meditates and smokes (not at the same time as far as I know), he hasn't an ounce of fat on him but eats everything going, especially buns. When I cooked roast beef for him he ate *all* the Yorkshire puddings – about eleven. He's forty years old and looks thirty.

As each role gets cast, the fact of the shoot becomes increasingly concrete. I rewrite scenes with the actors in my head. At the end of March I go away for two weeks, try to forget about the script and think about Elinor. This diary begins on the first day of rehearsals.

Friday 7 April

Shepperton Studios house the production offices and rehearsal rooms. We are working on one of the smaller stages where, last year, we filmed some interiors for *Carrington*. Rehearsals with Gemma and Kate. Both surprised to find that Ang begins with meditation and exercises – this is not usual. We sit on cushions and breathe. We massage each other's pressure points. It's very painful. Loud screams, particularly from Winslet.

I'm still doing rewrites in the evenings – small points to do with location and honing dialogue. There's always something. We're asked to do written homework for Ang. This is also unusual. he wants character studies and sets a list of questions, mostly addressing background and 'inner life'. Inner life is very important to him. Some actors react well to this, some don't. But we all do it. Imogen Stubbs (Lucy Steele) wins prize for best effort in the form of a letter to Elinor from Lucy some years after their respective marriages (see Appendices). Before casting began I remember saying to Ang that nothing mattered more than that every actor be funny. Very witty cast.

Our session with Jane Gibson (movement duenna and expert on all manners historical) is both revealing and rewarding. We learn the root and meaning of the bows and curtsies – or reverences, as Jane calls them. As you enter a room you 'cast a gladdened eye' about you. Beautiful phrase. It has boiled down over the centuries to mean a come-on. I remember my father once saying in a restaurant where I was flirting outrageously with one of the waiters, 'Stop giving that young man the glad eye.'

The bow is the gift of the head and heart. The curtsy (which is of course a bastardisation of the word 'courtesy') a lowering in status for a moment, followed by recovery. She speaks of the simplicity and grace of the time, the lack of archness. The muscularity of their physique, the strength beneath the ease of movement. She reminds us that unmarried women would not necessarily have known about the mechanics of sex. We search for a centre of gravity. Everyone suddenly feels clumsy and ungainly. As Jane says, we don't know how to behave any more.

Hugh Grant breezes in after last night's premiere of *An Awfully Big Adventure*, in Timberland boots and specs, a blue shirt. Repellently gorgeous, why did we cast him? He's much prettier than I am. It is Ang's first rehearsal with Hugh. He admits to being nervous – they both light up cigarettes. I watch, smugly non-smoking, but am soon to return to my old habit of rolling up my own.

Hugh: 'The moral of film-making in Britain is that you *will* be fucked by the weather.'

Ang says it's the only thing worrying him. His sang-froid is extraordinary. I think I must take up t'ai chi.

Cloudy. We shoot make-up and hair tests. My hair looks too red, Kate's make-up not quite right. We shoot more tests and solve the problems. Libby Barr, continuity (Scottish, sparky, vast collection of *outré* earrings), clanks away on an ancient typewriter. We work on with Jane Gibson. She's deliciously fierce with us. My concave chest is expanding outwards little by little.

Monday 10 April

Writing endless additional dialogue. This is to cover entrances and exits or wherever it's necessary for background chit-chat. Difficult for actors to extemporise in nineteenth-century English. Except for Robert Hardy and Elizabeth Spriggs, who speak that way anyway.

Jane reminds us that God is in his heaven, the monarch on his throne and the pelvis firmly beneath the ribcage. Apparently rock and roll liberated the pelvis and it hasn't been the same since. We all stand about like parboiled spaghetti being straightened out. I've covered the telly up, hidden the radio and cancelled all the newspapers. Hello, 1811.

Tuesday 11 April

No one can sleep for excitement. Costume designers John Bright and Jenny Beavan wish they had three more weeks but have done truly great work. The shapes and colours are inimitable. Lindsay's already in Plymouth frantically trying to cut the script. It's still too long. The art department object to us bathing Margaret in the parlour. Apparently they always used a kitchen or bedroom in the nineteenth century. Perhaps the Dashwoods are different, I suggest, unhelpfully.

Start to pack for ten weeks.

Thursday 13 April

Riding side-saddle is bizarre. Lesson with Debbie Kaye, who is in charge of training the actors to ride the horses and providing the carriages – everything to do with the transport of the times. It's a huge responsibility and great to find that it's a woman's. Quite unusual in this country. She put me on Small George, who was a bit skittish. The saddle has two leather protuberances. You wrap your legs around and hold on tight. Very good for the thighs. I wobble about, trying to be brave.

Monday 17 April

Our hotel, Alston Country House in Devon, is very grand and comfortable. We're here for six weeks to shoot the entire Barton Cottage and Norland Park sections and one interior scene in Mrs Jennings's London house. I'm in the top of the building, between eaves, rain and wind howling. No duvets but old-fashioned sheets and blankets and good tomato soup. England. Hugh Grant arrives tomorrow but I've nicked the prettiest room. Very low ceiling, so can't do Reebok stepping without knocking myself out.

Kate arrived looking slightly wild. Said her solo sessions with Ang had reduced her to a squashy bit of cotton wool. She's practising the piano on a keyboard in her room.

James Schamus and family are here. I gave their small

child an Easter egg. I am a creep. Quick dinner with them and Ang and his wife Jane who's visiting with the children for a while. We talked about her work as a microbiologist and the behaviour of the epithingalingie under the influence of cholesterol. She's fascinated by cholesterol. Says it's very beautiful: bright yellow. She says Ang is wholly uninterested. He has no idea what she does.

I check this out for myself. 'What does Jane do?' I ask. 'Science,' he says vaguely.

Laurie Borg turned up, a wild look in his eye. His girlfriend had left early because he's not interested in anything but getting *Sense and Sensibility* started. We're all at it . . . Long psychological investigations of character over dinner. Why does Morag (Ross, make-up designer) always wear black? Laurie thinks she's very spiritual. We all think Lindsay needs to work less hard. James finds the National Trust rather suspicious of us all. He's had to sign a contract – otherwise they would not have allowed us to start rigging at Saltram tomorrow. Which would mean no lights and therefore no shooting. I'm trying to adjust to new home life and family. Quite calm under circumstances. My nails and cuticles, however, are bitten to buggery.

Kate and I at dinner revert to girliness thus: 'Oh no no no I'm not eating, oh all right just a starter then, ooh that looks good, can I taste it, give it here then, are you going to finish that? christ no of course I can't have pudding bring four spoons, just an inch then, just to relax me, no don't take the bottle away it's a waste definitely no coffee do you have decaf?' etc. It's pathetic. I'm thirty-six and ashamed of myself.

My bathroom looks like the cosmetics department at Harvey Nicks. Aromatherapy oils mostly, which I never use. Tranquillity. Harmony. Anti-depression. Quiet time. Deep relax. Anti-stress. There's a shower attachment on the bath that does not bode well. Have invested in a ghetto blaster. Bunged on Handel's *Messiah* until I got depressed.

Bed with the script, Austen's letters, a sore back and wind. Inside and out.

Tuesday 18 April

Slept like the dead. Seared mouth on very hot porridge at breakfast with Lindsay. We discussed the 'novelisation' question. This is where the studio pay someone to novelise my script and sell it as *Sense and Sensibility*. I've said if this happens I will hang myself. Revolting notion. Beyond revolting.

Lindsay said that the executive she had discussed it with had said 'as a human being I agree with you – but . . .' I laughed until my porridge was cool enough to swallow.

Good-luck flowers arrived at home from Danny de Vito and Jim Sheridan. There's class for you. My mother has filched them. Sun's out. Off to get my roots dyed. Party tonight for the cast and crew to say hello. Yacht Club in Plymouth. I have no desire whatsoever to go but it's a good idea.

Kate looks a bit white. The bravest of the brave, that girl. I can't imagine what sort of a state I would have been in at nineteen with the prospect of such a huge role in front of me. She is energised and open, realistic, intelligent and tremendous fun.

Bought herbal teas – anti-stress, relax, quiet time, deep sleep etc. Did a work-out, bent double. Somewhat foxed by my new music machine – can't work out how to rewind tape. Nineteenth century clearly encroaching faster than I think.

9.30 p.m. Back from party. Crew were rigging and didn't really show till 8.30. But we tarted about and said hello to a few folk and they all seem great. Hugh Grant arrived. Slammed into a pint of bitter and some chicken goujons like nobody's business. I had a glass of water and tried to keep my hands off the scampi.

Morag showed me an eye-shadow container she'd bought for me. 'It's cosmic,' she said. I opened the lid and lo and behold, there was an Austen quotation: 'It was a delightful visit, perfect in being much too short.' A happy coincidence. I'm tired and must to bed.

Wednesday 19 April

Was up at six to a peerless sky and frost. Sunken roads are beautiful to behold and Devon lambs remarkably handsome. Arrived for the opening 'Big Luck' ceremony – a Buddhist ritual Ang observes at the beginning of every film. He had set up a trestle table with large bowls of rice, two gongs, incense sticks, oranges (for luck and happiness), apples (for safe, smooth shooting), a bouquet of large red-petalled flowers (for success) and an incongruous pineapple (for prosperity). Everyone lit a stick of incense, bowed in unison to the four corners of the compass and offered a prayer to the god of their choice. The camera was brought in on the dolly (which is a small wheeled platform on which the camera, operator and focus-puller sit) for a blessing, and a few feet of film were rolled. Ang struck the gongs, we all cheered and planted incense in the rice bowls. I cried. Al Watson, one of the electricians (or 'sparks'), passed Ang and said, 'Is this going to happen every day, guv?'

Rehearsals begin for Kate and Gemma's first scene – a difficult one to start with, very intimate and full of grief. They talk about Elinor's growing attachment to Edward and in her responses Marianne reveals her romantic sensibilities and sets up the image of her ideal man. We're also aware that behind Mrs Dashwood's equally romantic visions is a harder-edged reality – she must get her daughters married for their financial and social security. To find the balance between profound familiarity and informing the audience about character is hard. I'm very concerned not to allow ourselves any false affection – the sentimentalised 'close' family who are always caressing each other. I don't think they exist.

Neither Gemma nor Kate is sentimentalist, but still, it's always something to watch out for.

Margaret's tree-house is palatial. Not quite what I had in mind. Fabulous thing. The National Trust volunteers hover, watching us all like hawks. The welcome to Saltram was not the warmest. 'This house is much older than any of you and deserves your respect.' We all feel like a group of disreputable roadies. Clearly, they expect us to lay waste to the place. It is alarming, however, to see the sheer numbers of a film crew (about one hundred and twenty people) and the weight of equipment. The expressions on the faces of the volunteers veer between a diffident shyness and nervous terror as another jack-booted bruiser comes clanking in with large bits of metal that miss the precious mouldings by a whisker.

The sparks are, however, very respectful. I notice one tall blond, unreasonably handsome in an Aryan way, and poke Al Watson between the ribs. 'Who's *that*?' I ask.

'Paul Kemp,' he says. 'Yeah, I know. It's all his own, that hair, not dyed. We tease him something rotten, poor lad.'

'Well, it's always nice to have someone beautiful to look at,' I murmur.

'Not good enough for you, am I?' says Al, who then presses some of his wife's excellent bread pudding into my grasp. Al worked on *Carrington* last year. It's a small world.

Saltram is a wonderful house – but, like all that has been preserved and not used, has an empty atmosphere. I dare say we will soon see to that . . .

Chris Newman (the first assistant director, who controls the set) and I have been on five films together (*Much Ado*, *Howards End*, *Peter's Friends*, *Remains of the Day* and this) and he has always looked the same. A touch of Indiana Jones, felt trilby, khaki, long blond hair, bearded, with a low, authoritative voice.

Bernie Bellew is the second assistant director, who coordinates everything from the 'base' and is responsible for getting the actors to the set on time. Base comprises actors' trailers, hair and make-up buses, catering bus, toilets, construction and electrical vehicles, generators and so forth. Looks like backstage at a fairground. Bernie is a young, gentle man with blue eyes and hair that was already greying when I first met him on *The Tall Guy* in 1988.

Ben Howarth is our third AD. Tall, with a faraway look that belies his efficiency. He chases us all up and is constantly on the move as he listens to Bernie's instructions on his earpiece.

Rebecca (Becca) Tucker, the runner, is quintessentially English-rose with a sweetness of character to match and a firm hand. Runner is a good job description – she does everything at speed.

Three scenes down. Gemma and Kate triumphed and shook a lot all over. Nerve-wracking to do the first shot on anything. Hugh and I did Edward and Elinor talking and walking and got cold. The sun shone, everyone divested themselves of puffa-jackets. Then it hailed. I wondered about the Big Luck ceremony a bit after that, but Ang seemed quite pleased to have cloud. Paparazzi arrived for Hugh. We had to stand under a tree and smile for them.

Photographer: 'Hugh, could you look less – um – '

Hugh: 'Pained?'

My first director's note (criticism) from Ang: 'Very dull.' A bit of a blow. Then: 'Don't look so old,' which didn't help. But we've started. We're off. He was cock-a-hoop by the end of the day and no wonder since there were hardly any disasters. Lots of public watching, quietly interested.

Home 8 p.m. It took me two hours to remove make-up, have bath, make calls, eat a pear and light some relaxing candles. 'Night-time' teabags and anti-stress oil in the bath. None of it works; I'm zinging.

Thursday 20 April

Up 7 a.m. after a fractured night's sleep. Very cold. Found two lambs in the road, tried to get them back to their mother and failed horribly. Left them bleating ferociously at us from the middle of a bush. Porridge, toast and a large pot of tea during make-up. Sore hairpins, very long lighting job. Edward finds Elinor crying for her dead father, offers her his handkerchief and their love story commences. Ang very anxious that we think about what we want to *do*. I'm very anxious not to *do* anything and certainly not to think about it.

I've ink everywhere from practising with quills. Kate very calm and happier today, I think, now she's up and running. Indoors, thank God, all day.

The morning flew by with Hugh, who is as great an actor as I've always thought. So light and yet very much *felt*. He's made Edward rather troubled and halting, almost a stammerer. It's particularly good because it illustrates how relaxed he feels with Elinor, with whom he can be both funny and fluent.

Harriet (Walter) has chosen a dog for Fanny. It's pointy and shakes all the time. In her close-up we all had to wave cake at it to stop it staring into the camera or at its owner. Didn't faze Hat for one second, but the dog thought we were mad.

I've learned that Hugh and I caused Ang great suffering the other day. He has never had any actor question anything before. In Taiwan the director holds complete sway. He speaks and everyone obeys. Here, actors always ask questions and make suggestions. In this instance he'd designed a particular shot where Elinor and Edward walk through the gardens at Norland talking. Hugh and I were concerned about shooting (or 'covering') their expressions as there's so little time in which to see these people fall in love and the shot seemed too far off to capture them. In the event his idea was much better than ours, but that we should have had an idea at all came as a genuine shock and he was deeply hurt and confused. Better today, after Lindsay and James explained that these were perfectly normal working methods. We talked and I think he feels easier. I feel terrible – as though I've ruined Ang's first day by not being sensitive enough to his situation. It must have been terrifying – new actors, new crew, new country and then us sticking our oars in.

Chastening to realise yet again how much I have to learn about being too impatient and overwhelming. Bed in a heap of rubble.

Friday 21 April

Not much sleep. Demonised myself to such an extent last night I half expected to rise with two small horns. Wrote to Ang last night – this culture shock thing works both ways, it seems. Ang gave me a hug and said he was so touched by my letter he couldn't sleep. So we're all on course again but I am being cautious with my suggestions. I'm appalled to find that Emilie François (Margaret), who is twelve, is keen to 'lose a few kilos'. Does all that horror really start so young these days? I snorted a lot and forced a Jaffa Cake down her.

I'm freezing.

No dramas. Lindsay and James also suffering slight culture shock and a bit frustrated by the pace of things. Ang expects the ADs to be the tough ones and they expect him to be the tough one. So no one's tough and things move slowly. The beginning of a film is like watching a huge newborn centipede trying to get up on its hundred legs and go for a walk. Keeps tripping up until it's worked out how to coordinate. Any film will take two to three weeks to get into its stride – some never do. I think the key is good communications.

A care package arrived from Columbia Pictures: dressing gown, slippers, bath-pillow, blanket. A *care* package. Half expected a Zimmer frame (one of those balancing frames you get given when you're old and wobbly). Very kind. Caring, even.

Roast beef and a square of chocolate for lunch. Very yang. I keep tripping over my frock and swearing.

9 p.m. Alston Hall. Back after completing the day's work, no dramas. Terribly wound up. Adrenalin flowing. Difficult to sleep even after such long days. The hours vary – never less than twelve; today, fifteen. Ang very keen on the yin and yang of *Sense and Sensibility*. His sensibility very unsentimental, like Austen's. They're remarkably connected. She'd be astonished.

Sometimes there are eight or more National Trust volunteers in the room when we shoot, all in varying states of suspicion. The fire alarm went off. Fire engines came racing; we all rushed out on the gravel drive, everyone thinking it was us. In fact, one of the elderly residents of Saltram had left a pan on the oven in her flat. Apparently this happens all the time. The tenant in question is appearing as an extra – playing one of the cooks.

Huge spot on my cheek. Security guards for Hugh, poor soul. Ah, what it is to be a matinee idol and followed around by nutters.

Saturday 22 April

Cannot seem to sleep these days. Woke at 1 a.m. convinced it was time to get up. Back to bed with a scowl, a plum and Her Letters. Frantic dreams once I finally slept.

The hotel clearly switches central heating on late at weekends. Freezing at 6.30 a.m. and no hot water.

10.30 a.m. Pissing down with rain and very cold, which makes everyone depressed. Bought large bag of sweets which we all sucked noisily.

Sunday 23 April

1 a.m. Finally about to go to bed after hugely full and successful day. We've finished this period at Saltram without having dropped (filmspeak for having failed to cover something) a scene. A couple of shots had to go, but I don't think they'll be necessary. Ang very relieved. Mick Coulter (director of photography – Glaswegian, witty, perfectionist) and Phil Sindall (camera operator – shy, sensitive, patient) are pleased. It is an extraordinary achievement on all their parts, given the exigencies of the location. We'll return here in a few days and finish the Norland section.

Woke last night and sobbed for some reason. Relief, possibly.

Harriet and Gemma delivered excellent acting every time in dining-room scene. Theatrical training . . .

Hugh Grant bought us all drinks. We sat in the bar and played daft games – Lindsay is on excellent form. Rained all day. We froze.

Woke 7.30 after five hours, wrecked. Ate all day and sat in sun. We're all bright pink. Morag will kill me. Put pyjamas into laundry after only a week's wear and felt profligate.

Monday 24 April

New location: the front room of Mrs Jennings's London house is being shot on the Flete Estate, in the owner's home. The rest of Mrs Jennings's house will be shot in Salisbury. Most locations on film are a composite of several buildings – it's rare to find everything you need in one place, and Ang is very particular about the dimensions, colour and light in a room.

Lunchtime. Long rehearsal with Imogen Stubbs as Lucy, in the scene where Edward comes in and finds her with Elinor. There are eighteen set-ups. (Each shot is referred to as a set-up. We tend to shoot anything up to ten takes on every set-up. The number of the take is written on the clapperboard, or 'slate', and sometimes a shot will be called a slate.) It will take two days. Hugh won his Bafta for *Four Weddings* and was good in the scene. Bastard.

8.30 p.m. Home to Alston Hall. Raining. Soup, glass of wine. Very difficult scene and all a little tired but good concentration nonetheless. Four people in a room, each with entirely different motives and reactions to the same situation, requires a lot of coverage. Ang's taken to requesting what he calls 'smirks'.

'Endearing smirk, please' – which I find pretty tricky.

'Try rigorous smirk' – even trickier. I give it a go but end up going purple with the effort. Very little appetite.

Tuesday 25 April

Grey 6 a.m. We continue the scene. It's Hugh's close-up. After several takes, Ang said to Hugh, 'Now do it like a bad actor.'

Hugh: 'That was the one I just did.'

Ang holds his small hand to his face when anxious, a small crease on his brow.

Chris Newman turns forty. We all jeer. Corset has crushed my stomach to pulp. Studio happy with dailies (or 'rushes') – developed film which the directors, producers and sundry others watch at the end of the day. This is also rushed to the States so that all the executives responsible can check they're not throwing their money away . . . Sometimes actors watch rushes, if they're allowed by the director. Ang doesn't wish it. It makes no difference to me because I never watch them. The only time I did was on *The Fortunes of War* in 1987 – I wanted to resign, leave a note of apology and then kill myself.

I walk to work. Magic. Pheasants, cows, horizons. Fruit salad and toast, chocolate biscuit at eleven, bean and lentil curry, peas, spinach and rice, apple crumble and custard at lunch, three sandwiches at tea, no dinner – appetite clearly restored.

Hugh languid. I told him he had the stamina of a whelk. Felt we might all have done rather 'period' acting today. Most confused. But we finished the scene, a minor miracle. You don't expect to get nine set-ups in a day as each one requires a re-light. This is when the sparks take over the set and move lights about and the actors go away and gossip. It can take anything up to three hours. Mick and Phil a bit grey about the gills.

Wednesday 26 April

Finished at Flete with Elinor offering Edward the living at Delaford courtesy of Colonel Brandon. Very moving, the heartbreak beneath the courtesies, Edward's attempt to apologise, the great unspoken love between them. I couldn't get through the rehearsal without crying at the thought of losing someone so irrevocably . . . Did entire scene in four hours or less (five set-ups), not bad, and Hugh was great. I irritate him with all my hugs of affection but generally he's very sweet to me. Nice to be out of that room.

It's 3 p.m. and we're back at Saltram. Weather

changeable so it's possible we'll do the stables scene. Everyone knackered as dailies went on till midnight. Bit peeved, they all were. The material continues to satisfy so no problems as such. Lindsay wants more emotion, Ang wants less. Hugh wants quite a bit and I don't know who I am any more. Ang slowly accustoming himself to the way we work – he says English crews are slower but that is because there's more respect and the ADs don't yell at them like they do in America. I think he likes it.

We're not allowed to touch or move any of the furniture in Saltram, which makes for amusement. Today I saw an elderly lady, one of the volunteers (who are allowed to touch the furniture), being asked whether we could move an antique bench. She pushed her handbag firmly up her shoulder, picked up the bench and tottered off on high heels, watched by six strong grips and props men all completely bemused.

Bed 9 p.m. with script. Back on schedule. Two big scenes tomorrow. Getting quite nifty with a quill these days.

Thursday 27 April

Slept for nine hours! Time for a real breakfast. Small George (Elinor's horse) kept falling asleep under the lights in the stable and had to be poked regularly to keep his head up. Ang started to smoke in the stable, was advised against it – twice – and ran out, arms flapping, slightly bewildered.

Ang: 'In Taiwan, directors are allowed to do exactly what they want.' Then he giggled. Stood smoking in the rain and described how, in Taiwan, he would be followed about with chairs, ashtrays, wet towels, tea in constant attendance. We all stood about and looked at him and laughed.

The hotel has a wedding tonight so we're all off to another hotel in Plymouth for the night.

Friday 28 April

6 a.m. call. I woke at 2.30 and had a darkish time. Nice easy scene this a.m. but I feel unattractive and talentless. I look like a horse with a permed fringe. Did poetry-reading scene where Marianne teases Edward. Ate veg and rice.

Evening in the new hotel overlooking Sainsbury's car park. Back to the twentieth century with a vengeance. Took ages to get in with key card. Hate them. I like a proper key, which must mean something. Austen very keen on keys, I seem to remember. Hugh and I wondering if we're any good. Kate seems very well. Independent soul. She's taken herself off to see *Little Women*. This hotel is unspeakably lowering.

Saturday 29 April

Very fond of hotel. Slept like a log. Up 7.30. In to work, discussed the decision to put some of the actors in a different hotel to the rest of us, bad for morale, and also a party to be given Saturday 13th, good for morale.

Hugh G. says he finds the work very technical. I'm not quite sure what he means but I nod sympathetically. I feel the most appalling frump. Opened papers to find *The Tall Guy* and *Much Ado* advertised on the telly with casually rude remarks about them everywhere. Bit of a downer. Looking forward to some booze tonight and a decent meal with time to enjoy eating it. My body needs exercise but is holding up very well. No weight going on.

Found Ang asleep on set, folded up like a little dolly in his chair. Nice shot of Elinor and Edward walking while being watched by Fanny and Mrs Dashwood. All in one, nice and smooth. Last day at Saltram. Was going to give the National Trust boss lady a box of chocolates but I've eaten them.

Sunday 30 April

12.20 a.m. Soup and booze in bar. Finished at Saltram. Huzzah. Did very bad close-up at night, which didn't help my mood or fatigue, but Ang was philosophical. He doesn't indulge us but is always kind when we fail. A pleasant evening. I'm lonely.

8.20 a.m. Slept heavily from one to eight. Weary but calmer from a drinking night. Bath and then a walk with Kate before lunch. Praying for good weather for the wedding. Greg Wise (Willoughby) turned up to ride, full of beans and looking gorgeous. Ruffled all our feathers a bit.

7.30 p.m. Fantastic outing, sunny drives, five courses at Gidleigh Park Hotel and skinny-dipping in the river. I'm dyeing hair with Jan (Archibald, hair designer, exceptionally good woman). Helluva week ahead. Notes from Ang for Kate have floored her but she rallies. We all got them, I remind her.

Mick's joke: What's the difference between a pig and a grip? A pig won't spend the entire night trying to get the grip to go to bed with it. He swears this only applies to American grips but it's delightfully insulting either way. Richard Broome, our grip, is a perfect gentleman as far as I can tell.

Monday 1 May

Frumpy, sad, old and weepy today. New location. Caravans miles away. Ang patient, radiating calm. Hugh has taken to calling him 'the Brute'.

Later: Everyone hauling their way through the day. Kissing Hugh was very lovely. Glad I invented it. Can't rely on Austen for a snog, that's for sure. We shoot the scene on a hump-backed bridge. Two swans float into shot as if on cue. Everyone coos.

'Get rid of them,' says Ang. 'Too romantic.'

Now on horses, which is a bugger. Sheep and all. Very bolshie 'period' sheep with horns and perms and too much wool. If they fall over, they can't get up. Someone

has to help them. Can't be right. Ang wants sheep in every exterior shot and dogs in every interior shot. I've suggested we have sheep in some of the interiors as well.

Vehicles, mud, single-track roads. Impossible. Lovely weather so we are in great hopes of sun tomorrow. I feel without muscles today. Morag says we'll get through the week and bank holiday will give everyone a break.

Ang, after a particularly trying time with our flock (very quiet): 'No more sheeps. Never again sheeps.'

5.30 p.m. Very much cheerier. Just the strain of getting started again. Lovely scene on the horses, who were very well-behaved. That Debbie Kaye is a genius. Hugh and I did the first take completely out of character, we were concentrating so hard on riding and hitting our marks and not masking each other, etc. He turned into a champagne baron and I did something out of Sidney Sheldon. Got back on track afterwards but it just shows you. Gareth Wigan (Columbia executive and a great supporter of the project) arrived – seems very pleased. Kate and I did a quick shot on a hill. I'm in and out of hats, boots, pincurls, hairpieces, the corset and different frocks every ten minutes. Bitty day. Tomorrow will be difficult and exciting and everyone is on board. Entire cast, except Imogen and Richard Lumsden.

9.10 p.m. Bed. Imelda (Staunton) down from Inverness. Alan (Rickman) also just arrived, is in the bar with Hugh G., Mick and Kate.

Incipient thrush, me. Luckily Kate had some live

goat's yoghurt which I've applied with middling results. Ang told us about his early sex life today. 'So painful,' he said, then laughed a lot.

Tuesday 2 May

Woke sevenish after troubled night to thick mist. Tremendous excitement at Berry Pomeroy, the exquisite village where we are to shoot the wedding. And mist. We try to convince ourselves that it's an interesting idea to do the film's last joyous shot of Marianne and Brandon's wedding in thick mist.

'It's different,' says Lindsay.

'Sort of eastern,' I add, clutching at straws.

Wednesday 3 May

Yesterday a triumph, I think, and the most perfect weather imaginable. Mist left on cue. Found Ang having breakfast – two eggs, a kipper, a scone and some raspberry jam. 'What's so funny?' he said.

Greg on for his first day. It's like having a colt in the make-up caravan. Alan Rickman splendid in uniform. He and Kate look wonderful together.

Finished wedding. Happiness. Two cameras, ours and a steadicam (which is strapped to the body of the operator and offers more mobility), to cover the procession – much like a pantomime walk-down, actually – of Marianne and Brandon out of the church, followed by

Mrs Dashwood, Margaret, Elinor and Edward (who are supposed to be already married but I can't help feeling that it will look like a double wedding. Depressing thought – too neat) . . . Mrs Jennings and Sir John, the Palmers, John and Fanny. It's Alan's first day and his last appearance in the movie. Rather confusing.

'*You* try it,' he said darkly. 'I haven't played a scene yet and I'm already married and being followed by you lot . . .'

He's suspicious about what everyone's getting up to behind his back but I assure him we're all behaving very well and trying not to go over the top. Local children appear as extras – I chat them up. They've all got names like Jacob, Saul and Abraham. Hugh G. naps on the church pews between takes. A peacock sits in the tree opposite the church and makes its mournful cry all day.

Thursday 4 May

Organising the party. Cheerier. Lisa Henson (head of production at Columbia) rang yesterday just as we were watching Greg drive the curricle (a high-flyer specially constructed for the shoot. Bright yellow with black wheels. Sexy contraption) at speed up a hill – very dangerous. We buggered the sound of the end of the shot by cheering. Odd watching that in the dying afternoon light as Lisa chatted from a morning Columbia in LA. Dailies are pleasing them – relief all round. Electronic Press Kit on set. I get very ratty. Don't like being watched by another camera. It's background material and interviews that will be used for the press later, so very necessary.

Caught sun through my costume, it's like the Bahamas. Watched all morning, didn't get on camera. Everyone in high spirits. The girls discuss the indefensible behaviour of some men who will parade their obscenely large beer bellies without a qualm and then comment brainlessly if a woman eats a bun. Make-up trailer has become very militant.

Had lunch with Alan in his trailer and talked about theatre. He was as much put off by two years in *Les Liaisons Dangereuses* as I was by fifteen months in *Me and My Girl*. I like *evenings* too much. I'm not sure all that repetition is good for you . . .

Ang's note to Alan: 'More subtle: do more.' Alan flummoxed but only momentarily. I am constantly astounded by Ang – his taste is consummate. It sometimes takes a while to work out exactly what he wants but it's always something subtler. Try to picture myself working in Taiwan. Imagine the loneliness.

Very hot today. 9.30 p.m. and I'm off to bed. Did small scene between Elinor and Mrs Dashwood. No time, no concentration, no light and all sorts of emotional difficulty. Ang spot on with his notes – we started very hot and ended up far calmer and more flowing. Vast numbers of midges bit us and moved into Gem's wig – wind machine kept them at bay. Crows cawed like buggery – we fire a shotgun just before the take, which

shuts them up for a few minutes. Who says the country is peaceful? Ang misses the motorway.

Friday 5 May

9 a.m. Just finished line-up for Hugh's last scene ('My heart is and always will be yours'). Peerless weather. Hugh on good form.

Ang to Hugh: 'This is your big moment. I want to see your insides.'

Hugh: 'Ah. Right-o. No pressure then . . .'

I'm slightly tense – big crying explosion to do next.

Later: Tenser than fuck now, as the morning's work only prepared me and we'll do my shots this afternoon. Make-up bus is like a sauna – it all melts off as you apply it. Went and requested air-conditioning units. Ang wanted a difficult shot this a.m. and Mick talked him out of it (he felt there wasn't enough time) and then felt a bully. It's easy to feel a terrible bully with Ang –but things are improving, I think.

Hugh G. has finished. He appears on set looking completely out of place in his boots and the shirt he was wearing on the first day of rehearsals.

'I'll miss you,' I say weepily.

'No, you won't,' he says.

He's quite right, of course, there's no time for all that. He walks off to say goodbye to everyone and that's the last I see of him.

10.30 p.m. Finished at 9.30 and am rewriting tomorrow's scene. It's too complicated for the time we have available to shoot it, needs simplifying.

Saturday 6 May

A very ancient lot this a.m. Lots to do but Lindsay and I cut the Thomas scene a little and smoothed out the arrival of the piano so I hope we'll get it all. Packed a bag for the weekend, determined to be off as soon as possible. The house representing Barton Cottage is also on the Flete Estate, and one of the most beautiful spots we've ever seen. Takes the curse off a six-day week.

Sunday 7 May

Gidleigh Park Hotel. Here for a weekend off. Walked to Dartmoor, among black-faced lambs and foals, climbed to the top of a large rock and met a small boy.

Me: Hello.

Boy: H'llo.

Me: This is a good place, isn't it?

Boy: Yes.

Me: If it weren't hazy we could see for miles.

Boy: On a clear day you can see way over to south Devon.

Pause.

Boy: That's something you can't buy.

At which point I expected him to sprout wings and

ascend to heaven. He was wearing a slightly disappointing AC/DC T-shirt, though, which brought me back to earth.

Tuesday 9 May

Changeable weather. It was peerless at 6.30 a.m. so we got ready to do the picnic – which meant Luci (Arrighi, production designer and the most elegant woman on earth) and the art department had to change the front of the cottage to the later, lived-in look. Removing treehouse etc. took ages. Now broken clouds have arrived, which means shooting everything in both cloud and sun. This is tricky for Mick in particular. Everyone rushes in and out with polystyrene and flags, and Terry (Edland, head electrician or 'gaffer') gazes at sun through his dark glass shouting, 'Sun in about three minutes' – so we shoot a take in cloud first, and then the sun comes out halfway through and we have to stop and start again. This happens all day. Chilly. I issue direful warnings against whimsy in these love scenes. The picnic is a wonderful Luci creation. Exquisite. It looks like it's being given by the Rothschilds. I ask Luci to take away pies and cakes and fruits and all the glory. 'Cheese, bread, apples and beer,' I say. 'They're poor.'

Luci makes a plea for the pork pie. 'They could have had it in the larder,' she wails as her divine portrait is dismantled.

I am unrelenting.

We may have to hire cheaper sheep. They're not close enough for their perms to register.

4.45 p.m. Rather nippy now. Lazy picnic atmosphere. Gunshots to shut the crows up. Partridges squawk, swans fly flappily over the estuary. It's noisier than the M25. Drink tea in green room. Art department busy with the interior – glorious colours, like a Dutch painting, washed out.

9.15 p.m. Home, constipated, to a glass of water and a handful of peanuts.

Wednesday 10 May

Weather now so changeable on all fronts that the call-sheet contains more options than a pizza menu. Different scenes proposed for the following conditions:

1. Bad weather (light wind)
2. Bad weather (strong wind)
3. Goodish weather
4. Good weather
5. Grey, still weather.

It looked like bad weather (light wind) when I rose at dawn. Checked call-sheet, which confirmed that the scene to be shot in these conditions didn't contain Elinor. Ha, I thought, and went back to sleep. Bernie rang at 8.20: 'We don't need you.' Ha, I thought and went back to sleep. Finally smoozled out at 9.45 and ordered porridge, which I ate in bed with a bit of jam. I was in heaven.

Got up and went to visit the set with Gemma. Everyone in wet-weather gear looking resigned. Mist machine extraordinary – a cylindrical contraption on a truck expelling great billowing clouds which were then pushed up the hill by the (light) wind. Nick (Wilkinson, horsemaster) did stunt riding for Greg brilliantly. Big George (Willoughby's horse) is stupendous. Another specially trained horse stands in to do the rearing.

Emilie soaked to the skin and frozen all day. I gave her an aromatherapy bath afterwards. Kate rolled down the hill endlessly, happily doing all her own stunts. Rain machine. Then it *did* rain so poor crew stood about in both special effects and real rain. Everyone sodden by the end of the day and exceedingly tired. I, on other hand, had dinner and sat up talking to Alan and Gemma. A real treat.

Cannes schedule for *Carrington* (which will open at the Festival) looks punishing so I'm trying to get it changed. Bit too much on, really. Or at least for me – I can't concentrate on more than one thing at a time. Bed at midnight after lots of wine but it doesn't matter because I have a day off tomorrow – incredible.

Friday 12 May

Bernie rang at 7.30 a.m. Sun's out. Got to work. Omigod. Stare at wine-sodden eyes in mirror and hate myself.

Willoughby arrives with Marianne. Ang said the rehearsal was too hectic – and that he's been bitten by scenes like this before. So busy that the audience just switches off. He's very interesting on the flow of energy in a film. Always thinks of everything in its widest context.

Wild a.m. trying to work out the blocking. Kate and Greg sopping wet and brave. Set up a shot that was designed only to go to a certain point in the scene but as Ang didn't cut we just carried on. At the end of the scene Phil said the lens was too pushed to contain anything but Ang said he'd just been watching the story – and he hadn't cut simply because he'd been enjoying himself. 'Try not to get into the habit,' said Linds, worrying about film stock and costs. Later, Ang said that he wanted the camera to watch the *room*, sense the change in it that a man, that sex, had brought. For Ang, the house is as important a character as the women.

Bed knackered at 10 p.m. Very wet people. Very cold. Cannes looking threatened. A good day, really – but there's so much to do. Paranoid delusions and loneliness struck at me so I must wise up and get to bed earlier.

Saturday 13 May

Up 6 a.m. to cloudless sky. Walked to work. Jan tells me I have to go to Cannes – she was very clear about it. I'll regret it if I don't, even if it wrecks me.

Alan R., who has clepped himself Colonel Weathercover ('weathercover' means interior scenes that are slated to be shot if the weather is not right for the scheduled exterior scenes) and spent days on end trying to amuse himself in the hotel, is in to work finally and looking a tad bewildered. 'I'm not as well as I would like to be,' he responded to my enquiry.

Greg very energetic this morning.

Morag: 'Nothing that a syringe of horse sedative won't cure.'

Overheard later:

Kate: 'Oh God, my knickers have gone up my arse.'

Alan: 'Ah. Feminine mystique strikes again.'

Sun went in and out all day so again we had to cover the scene in shine and cloud. Alan had a trying morning – trotting up, dismounting, tying up the bloody horse, dealing with his crop, taking his hat off and reverencing on the side of a hill. Horse kept moving around so its great black arse overwhelmed the shot. Deb Kaye lay on the grass, hissing at it, 'Get back, you bastard' etc. Not Alan's happiest moment but he was splendid, charming and virile.

Lots of argument about Willoughby's arrival. Should it all be on a master (i.e. one shot only)? The crew want coverage. Ang thinks coverage is irrelevant. Should Willoughby help Marianne into the carriage, or Brandon, or both? Should Marianne say, 'Now I shall really be able to play for you, Willoughby' or is it too rude and should she address it to the whole group? In the meantime, Greg has to drive in a carriage with two horses, make them stop on a pre-arranged mark, hold them steady while acting and getting Kate into her seat and then move them off as if he did such things every day of his life. Also the horses have taken to letting off lengthy and noisome farts during the takes. Debbie says it's the Devon oats. Privately I decide to lay off the porridge. Deb's as embarrassed for the horses as if they were her own children.

Kate tells me her first note from Ang was, 'You'll get better.' I shrieked.

It's raining now. The weather reports are all contradictory and none describes with any accuracy the weather we've got. Greg and Kate in the high-flyer were a wonderful sight – genuinely transported with excitement. Probably because it's quite dangerous.

We've yet to pick up the beginning of the scene in cloud. Given up now and have come inside to do at least one set-up on the hair-cutting scene with Gemma (where Willoughby begs a lock of hair from Marianne). Sat chilled, looking at the swans and cormorants flying over the estuary. We've flattened all the grass on the lawn and it has to be fluffed up for the shot. Hilarity reigns. I feel tired and out of it and beg not to do the scene tonight. But we have to do the scene – schedule is biting. I play the scene tired and out of it. Ang likes it.

Sunday 14 May

6 p.m. We await tea. There is a special weekend of 'miniature bear making' going on in the hotel. Apparently a group of ladies meet regularly for nice swims, meals, conversation and a shared interest in miniature bear making. Still trying to get my mind round it.

The party on Saturday was wild. Everyone fell on the opportunity to let go and was drunk before having drunk anything. Alan nearly killed me, whirling me about the place. Everyone was under the table by midnight except Greg, who was on the ceiling. I discussed the film industry with some of the drivers – who've seen it all, of course, and get very depressed about the fact that we don't finance nearly enough films in Britain. This film was financed in the States and most of the revenue will end up there. Ridiculous state of affairs. Had a bop with Ang. Very good dancer. 'I haven't done this for years,' he said, looking surprised and bouncing about like a piece of India rubber.

Home at 3.30 a.m. in a taxi, arseholed. I stumbled into my bedroom where Harriet Walter (who'd come down specially and was sharing my room) was already asleep. She sat bolt upright.

'Help me!' I wailed.

'Oh, God,' she said. 'Why don't you try throwing up?'

A good line in that cut-glass accent, I thought, even as I threw myself at the loo bowl.

Ang's latest note to Greg: 'Great acting. I think.'

Monday 15 May

Everyone looking slightly bushed. Up 6 a.m., looked at the sky, couldn't decide what it was going to do, so washed and went back to bed. Bernie rang and told me to stay in bed, then rang back twenty minutes later and said, 'Come in.' It's sunny, finally.

Alan R. in slight state of shock about working methods but I have assured him it works. We seem to feel our way into the shots. Ang's style of leadership is somehow to draw us all to him silently and wait for things to happen. He has the shape of shots in his head always and will stand for silent minutes on end thinking through the flow of the scenes to see if what we're doing will fit his vision. I find it very inspiring but it's quite different to being told what to do. More collaborative. I think he's enjoying our ideas more now he knows they don't present a threat or a lack of respect.

5.30 p.m. Going outside to catch the last of the daylight for Willoughby and Brandon's meeting, then coming back in for Alan's close-up. Strange to have Alan and Robert Hardy on board now, it feels like a new movie. Hugh's section seems months ago and another life. There are so many different story lines in this script and we've been entirely focused on Elinor and Edward. Now Brandon's story begins. Robert Hardy brings the nineteenth century with him, he's born out of his time. Courteous, intelligent and witty in tweed. I very much like the fact that there are four generations represented in this film – from Margaret's twelve-year-old perspective through Elinor and Marianne's twenties and Mrs Dashwood's forties to Mrs Jennings's sixties. Not a thirty-something in sight.

Ang massaged my stupid neck (stiff as wood from dancing too long). Taking a long time to get up to speed today.

Tuesday 16 May

10 a.m. At last the weather's broken! Couldn't sleep last night so I'm very grateful not to be on camera today. Up at nine to do a workout, eat porridge despite fear of flatulence and join them in the rain.

Later: Lots of very cold, wet people in real rain, effects rain and mist again. Slow start. Laurie's pulling his hair out.

Ang's gentle flow doesn't seem so gentle when you're frozen but all's well. Good humour prevails. I am in very fetching white wet-weather trousers and wellies. Look as if I work in a chicken factory. This was the day a very sodden Greg bounded up to Alan and asked, with all his usual ebullience, how he was. Long pause as Alan surveyed him through half-closed eyes from beneath a

huge golfing umbrella. Then – 'I'm dry.' Sometimes Alan reminds me of the owl in Beatrix Potter's *Squirrel Nutkin*. If you took too many liberties with him I'm sure he'd have your tail off in a trice.

10.20 p.m. In bed with a herbal cushion from Kate. She fainted at 6 p.m. – so cold, so wet for so long. Alan found Ang sitting on a box, his head low, his fists clenched.

'I tortured her,' he moaned.

'Don't worry,' said Alan. 'You'll have the opportunity to do it to me soon.'

Kate was sent flowers by the production and four bottles of Newcastle Brown Ale from the ADs. We warmed her up slowly in her caravan, her feet thrust into Greg's armpits. According to Paul (our paramedic) this is the best way of warming feet and she made a very good recovery. The hotel had built an enormous fire which we sat around with a glass.

Robert Hardy had had the day off and found an entrancing post office in Yealmpton that he could barely tear himself away from. 'A proper English post office smelling of dust and jam with a little old lady who enquired after my health.'

Elizabeth Spriggs has arrived. Full of energy, pouring out affection like a particularly comforting teapot.

Bad weather means more rain work for Kate tomorrow so we'll have to be very careful. We sat today in a strange, tiny hut on the beach, drying her stockings

before a real fire, and steaming gently. Good work today, though. Willoughby's entrance through the mist on a white horse. We all swooned. Ang laughed at us.

'This scene is ridiculous,' he said.

'It's a girl thing,' Lindsay and I replied.

Really wet, though, that rain.

Wednesday 17 May

Up 5.45 – looked at sky. Couldn't work it out. Washed. Walked to work. They cancelled me. Came home. Went back to bed at 7 a.m. and slept till ten – out like a light. Off to the set now, to watch Robert Hardy, who looks like a caterpillar in his costume.

Later found Ang looking at the estuary with a mournful expression. I went and stood beside him. After a moment he said, waving towards the water, 'Tide goes in, tide goes out, tide goes in, tide goes out – and still no sex.'

'Do you miss it?' I enquired, after I'd stopped laughing.

He nodded sadly. His family won't be back for weeks.

Kate got rained on again. She's been a total hero and heartbreaking on the hill with the sonnet. Alan arrived and had to run up a very steep hill in thick tweeds and thermals. Then he had to stand in rain which was blinding today. Thank God we had wind and clouds.

Thursday 18 May

Managed to pee on most of my underwear this morning (trailer loos are very cramped) so I'm in a very bad temper. Didn't sleep. Had three breakfasts to make up for it. Sun is out. Amazing that the cloud held just for those two days.

Robert and Liz come down to rehearse their arrival scene. Wonderful as they can extemporise within the period. Quick rewrite on arrival scene and we've got the line in about camphor being good for 'the staggers' so I'm pleased.

1.30 p.m. Good morning. Six horses, three carriages, six dogs, six actors – madness. All waiting for cloud. Thank God for Liz and Robert who are not only brilliant but stalwart. My bowels are up to no good today. There would appear to be several more scenes on the call-sheet. Help. Poor Emilie had a headache and a maths test today. It's hell being twelve. This week has flown. Some fight starting up over a Jaffa Cake in make-up.

7 p.m. Still shooting. Alan and Greg swanned in after a fabulous day visiting an English winery and pubs. We all spat at them. The sun has come out so we'll work indoors and go outside later. Rehearsing poetry-reading scene also.

8 p.m. Am slightly hysterical now. Huge spot has appeared on chin.

10.30 p.m. Finally in bed – far too late.

Friday 19 May

Woke 3.30. Well and truly bollocksed.

10 a.m. Already have a couple of things in the can, shot outside in the sun. Rain came on and we moved indoors.

Ang had a go on a horse. 'This is easy,' he said as it walked very sedately along, being led by Deb. *Sense and Sensibility* signs litter Devon – arrows with *S & S* on. Whenever Ang sees a B & B sign he thinks it's for another movie.

We're working on the second scene between Willoughby and Marianne where they read the sonnet together. Difficult to give poetry reading a sexy hue in this day and age but what else can he do? Give her a massage? Must avoid twee. Oh, please don't let any of it be twee, I'll die. I'll be assassinated by the Jane Austen Society (who rang James's company in New York to complain about the casting of Hugh Grant as Edward – too good-looking apparently).

My spot has gone volcanic and I'm very bitter about it.

6 p.m. Found myself, on the turnaround of the poetry-reading scene, acting my bit while tiptoeing about among mike leads, climbing over Chris (Gurney, boom operator, very stoic individual), putting props down on plastic beer boxes and picking up others, squeezing myself in beside the polystyrene and thinking, What the hell am I doing? I dare say a spot of alienation's good for you.

We all started singing 'Kumbaya' this p.m., which shows how tired we were – no one had the strength to put an end to it.

I received a wonderful invitation from a local couple with a very enjoyable sentence which ran thus: 'In particular there would be no question of anyone being advised of your being entertained here as this part of the country is famous for shellfish.'

Gemma (*to me as I scribble*): 'I do hope this diary isn't going to be libellous.'

Gemma is magic. She looks so innocent and pure and then she opens her mouth and says something rude. She's got the dirtiest laugh I've ever heard. Lindsay came into the green room the other day and asked her if she'd like a bun.

'I'd like a bun almost as much as I'd like a man,' she replied, unblinkingly.

Can't get my lenses in and grope blindly about the set.

Saturday 20 May

Cannes. Get on plane 9 a.m. – apparently it belongs to Chris de Burgh. My spot has made a third appearance and practically has features of its own. I try to improve my appearance and just end up getting a quantity of mascara in my hair. Press ahead.

7 p.m. Cannes rather quiet. They have less money from the government this year, I'm told. Pamela Anderson causing great excitement in black leather get-up. Went

for a walk despite earnest pleas from the publicity folk not to: 'You'll be bothered by photographers and public,' they intone. Trotted off down the Croisette and no one took a blind bit of notice except one young person who clutched her companion and hissed, 'Is that Sharon Stone?' I was thrilled until I realised she was referring to the woman behind me (who didn't look like Sharon Stone either). Charming journos all day. Foreign.

Sunday 21 May

Bad press conference on balance – useless questions and we weren't as entertaining as we might have been – but everything else went according to plan.

2 a.m. Finally in bed. The MTV party is opposite my hotel on beach so I'm buggered. Wax earplugs and pills the only answer. What a day. Screening went very well and Chris Hampton was pleased so everyone's happy. Didn't drink too much. Was got at by the fashion police for wearing jeans on the Marches of the Palais. I had no idea there was a dress code . . . Came home to an appalling review in *Variety*.

Monday 22 May

Up early to leave. Walked out of my bedroom to find my fat face outside every bedroom door on the Cannes *Newsletter*. A surreal and essentially unpleasant moment.

Tuesday 23 May

Bizarre to be back at Alston Hall. French press on *Carrington* very good. English press mixed but a good response in general and Polygram are very pleased. Press conference yielded the usual crop of daftness. I've been asked if I related personally to Carrington's tortured relationship with sex and replied that no, not really, I'd had a very pleasant time since I was fifteen. This elicited very disapproving copy from the Brits. They're like a pack of maiden aunts sometimes – slingbacks clacking and knitting needles pointing. No wonder people think we don't *have* sex in England.

Very fine rehearsal. Beautiful day. Stiff neck. Going great on atlas-arriving sequence. Emilie has a natural quick intelligence that informs every movement – she creates spontaneity in all of us just by being there. Generally a marvellous piece of direction from Ang, who loves the unspoken undercurrents everywhere.

We had to wait a lot for wind. It blew our skirts and aprons, and the coats hanging in the doorway. Something nostalgic, lonely about it.

Wednesday 24 May

Asleep by eleven with the help of a pill, up at six to cloud, no idea what we're doing, it changes by the moment. Fruit, toast, coffee. Ang has an upset stomach and has stopped eating pink iced buns for breakfast. His colon is grumbling. We talk about what he wants to do next. He longs for something masculine – opium wars, we suggest. Lots of men and guns.

Lunchtime. Kate and Gemma are sitting in their corsets talking about the Hollywood Porn Awards – they've found pictures of this ceremony in an old magazine. We've still not shot the master (the set-up that captures an entire scene or a large part of it. Then you cover the scene in close-up, two-shots and so forth).

Gemma, after two hours' waiting: 'Oh, God, it's like childbirth. You go on and on and on and on and still nothing happens.'

Twoish. Exhausted now and I get dizzy spells because my blood pressure has plummeted. Somewhat demoralised to have achieved only one shot by this hour. Everyone's yawning. A nine-hour break is really insufficient, but we generally get ten or twelve. This does not apply to many of the crew, though – de-rigging or prep for the next day's work can mean they get eight or nine hours off at most. The tired mood is right for this scene, though. Sun's out now so everyone's running around with filters, screens and heavy frowns. Very hard going today.

9.30 p.m. We didn't quite get to Gem's last shot, which upset her. Very frustrating after such a long wait. The ADs sent a bottle of champagne to the hotel in apology. She doesn't drink so we nicked it.

Thursday 25 May

Slept well for the first time in days and without pills. Bits and bobs today and wholly reliant on weather. Picking up this and that as we can, rather confusing. A sheep collapsed from heat exhaustion. Just keeled over in the back of shot. The shepherd's worrying about his flock and is always asking when he can shear them. After this we told him to go ahead. They appear later, with haircuts, behind Marianne and Margaret as they walk.

Friday 26 May

Lovely relaxed evening last night, clouds scudding across sky. An odd day, with a confusing number of scenes, plus doctors and acupuncturists for my neck and Mick's back. Everyone went in and out of the green room as various consultations took place. Plus a fair bit of snoozing. Rain. Winding down, mellow atmosphere. It will be like starting yet another movie next week. Am munching ham sandwiches. Robert Hardy left a crate of champagne. We live for pleasure. I've done nothing but eat all day. Morag said I was getting thin in the face. Fell asleep in Kate's lap. Feel very calm. Odd. Ang still off the buns and the smokes. We need some sun.

Later: Ang sitting shredding a polystyrene cup with a little frown creasing his smooth brow. Second unit are doing carriage run-bys (shots on moving carriages with no artists, although Roy Bond, one of the drivers, is

standing in for Mrs Jennings. He's the same shape but
has a large moustache. It won't read). All the girls from
hair and make-up are doing tapestries. It started with
one or two but has spread like wildfire – they're all at it
now. Most peculiar.

Lindsay comes in with the silhouette scene typed up. I
think it's good. We need more dialogue for Sir John and
Mrs Jennings as they walk up the path. Ironically that's
one of the bits I cut down as it was almost three pages. I
remember, back in the mists of pre-production, saying,
'They'll do it very quickly,' which cut no ice at the time.

Kate makes a bracelet. We're in our nighties, our
plaits down our backs. Ang settles down for a snooze.
The weather does worry him. Only one day left at this
location. Hypnotic, Kate's hands knotting the threads.

Shrieks of laughter ooze up from downstairs. Ang
asks about theatre – how anyone can do eight shows a
week for months on end. Nightmare visions of *Me and
My Girl* hove into left-hand side of brain. Thank God
there's no tap-dancing in this film. The green room full
of biscuits, buns and half-eaten sarnies, plus Monday's
newspapers. Ang under such enormous pressure I'm
surprised his colon hasn't crawled out of his mouth,
never mind grumbling. Discussion about shots and us
(Kate and I) sometimes looking less than perfect. Ang
says, that's not what it's about, looking good. We agree,
fervently. Typical mid-term reactions settling in – Paul
the medic rushing about supplying vitamins, laxatives,
herbal sleeping pills, aspirin and God knows what else.

Said goodbye to everyone at Alston Hall this a.m., which made us sad. I was so relaxed there I took to removing my make-up in the bar, sitting cross-legged in socks and leaving little damp pads of cotton wool everywhere. Disgusting, when you come to think of it. The staff looked after us like family.

We try to find an extra line for Margaret as she picks up Willoughby's gear in the rain. Lindsay suggests, 'I'll get the stuff,' which makes me laugh immoderately.

I counter with Willoughby saying, 'Pray get the stuff.'

'It's in the book!' we keep screaming.

Lindsay is having a horrid time of it. There's so much left to shoot. She's made a list of 'luxury' scenes and 'crucial' scenes. We almost didn't shoot Elinor listening to Marianne packing and deciding not to tell her about Lucy's engagement. Did it in the end, hoping it will be effective in one shot. Tempers fray. Candles are difficult to work with.

Saturday 27 May

Up 5.15 a.m. thinking, packpackpack. I appear to have accumulated more things. How does this happen? I haven't shopped. Think my bath oils have bred.

It's raining and dull and exactly the sort of weather we don't need. Will reshoot the Dashwoods' reaction to Edward's arrival ('I do not think it is Colonel Brandon') in the rain. Will it match the interior? Probably not. This is where Mick works magic and creates false sunlight. His concentration is terrific.

Ang must be getting better. He produced a lot of Chinese snacks for us last night – crunchy peas and freeze-dried cuttlefish.

Fell asleep at lunch and awoke to find Emilie, Kate, Ang and Greg playing games. It's not like work at all today. I'm *not* working, of course, but it doesn't feel as if anyone else is either. Ribald laughter floating up from the garden where the sparks are clearing away. Raining. Cosy.

Shooting Willoughby carrying Marianne up the path. They did it four times. 'Faster,' said Ang. They do it twice more. 'Don't pant so much,' said Ang. Greg, to his great credit, didn't scream. The image of the man carrying the woman is horribly effective. Male strength – the desire to be cradled again? Had sage discussion with John Jordan (focus puller, very gentle) over the barrel of the lens about allowing all those politically incorrect desires their head. I'd love someone to pick me up and carry me off. Frightening. Lindsay assures me I'd start to fidget after a while. She's such a comfort.

My roll-ups keep going out. Kate makes hers like small sleeping bags. It's impossible to imagine not leaving this place a mass of polystyrene cups and cables. But we will. The art department has added so much in the way of lintels, outside and in, shelves, plastering etc. that it's not easy to picture how it will look in its civilian state.

The estuary very Turneresque today. Soft air. Doing wild tracks for sound now – we all sit quietly as Tony Dawe (sound recordist, merry, keeps hens) records atmosphere and the odd line or two that we haven't managed to get 'clean' during the take.

Ang must be getting better. He's eating pickled cucumbers out of a tin.

Tuesday 30 May

Weekend in London. Tea, mooching, Chinese food; fought my way through the garden and then the mail. Travelled Monday with Kate and Imelda to Yeovil and found myself in a glory of stone and wisteria at Montacute – the location for Cleveland, home to the Palmers. The move of location has energised the troops, although a weekend always leaves people looking shell-shocked. We're five and a half weeks in with six and a half to go. The time shoots by. I determine to savour every precious moment daily and of course in the very nature of it there's almost no time to savour anything.

Talked about the long Brandon confession scene with Alan. The trick is to break up the bulk of the information with character and to make it a scene about – as Alan puts it – a man thawing out after having been in a fridge for twenty years. The movement of blood and warmth back into unaccustomed veins is extremely painful. The scene has existed in many different forms – flashbacks, stylised imagery – until I realised it was emotionally more interesting to let Brandon tell the story himself and find it difficult.

We're already juggling with the weather as it's going to improve and we need to do the exterior shots at Cleveland in grey at least.

4 p.m. Back to hotel (which is a glorious place called Summer Lodge in Evershot) after having done nothing but rehearse a little, dye my roots with Jan and eat. The Cleveland section of the story is fragmented anyway – and our days will reflect that.

Wednesday 31 May

Glorious sunshine. Hugh Laurie has arrived, which is a great fillip. There is no one on the planet who could capture Mr Palmer's disenchantment and redemption so perfectly, and make it so funny. He's writing a novel in between takes, in his trailer.

We prepare to do, 'I think Marianne may need a doctor.' Hugh surprised to learn that it's at night. 'Have you read the script?' I enquired tartly. Recalled Hugh Grant's words – 'I'm never acting with the screenwriter again.'

It's true I'm always at them. The language in the novel is complex and far more arcane than in the later books. In simplifying it I've tried to retain the elegance and wit of the original and it's necessarily more exacting than modern speech.

Spoke to Christopher Hampton, who's very pleased

about *Carrington* and tells me it's doing great business in France.

Three interior scenes today. Thank God we did Friday's work yesterday – weather seems set to improve. Spoke to Stephen Fry, who sounds very cheerful and is driving back across the States. Once, last year, my computer scrambled the script and because I am a computer-illiterate fool, I had no back-up. No one from Apple Mac could rescue it so I took it over to Stephen's and he spent an entire day finding it. I hyperventilated with gratitude for weeks.

Tourist saw Alan and said, 'Oh, look, there's Tom Cruise.' Probably the same one who thought I was Sharon Stone.

9.30 a.m. Still not shooting. Late start again. They refused to let us use the breakfast room yesterday so we re-set the scene of waiting for Dr Harris's diagnosis in a great hall, which changed the nature of the scene entirely. Quite good really, because it's tenser. It's perhaps better for suspense that the Palmers are more nervous than I've suggested in the script.

Mick's lighting for me coming downstairs with a candle was very complex. Tried the false candle with wires and batteries strapped in a bum-bag round my waist, the switch for it trapped between the cheeks of my arse, and realised it wasn't going to work. Hugh L. had his first spoken syllable and got very anxious. It's very hard starting one's part in the middle of a shoot.

Kate and I are on so consistently that we've forgotten the camera's there. Best thing.

National Trust very strict with their hours – but very nice people who actually seem quite pleased to see us.

Ang is in heaven. There is no dialogue. 'This is pure cinema,' he says, pleased.

I seem finally to have stopped worrying about Elinor, and age. She seems now to be perfectly normal – about twenty-five, a witty control freak. I like her but I can see how she would drive you mad. She's just the sort of person you'd want to get drunk, just to make her giggling and silly.

Ang is thrilled with all the topiary in the gardens. He had Marianne walking by this extraordinary wiggly hedge. Apparently it snowed one year and the snow froze the hedge. When the thaw came, they cut away the dead bits and continued to grow the hedge – in the shape of a wild snowdrift. It looks like a brain. 'Sensibility,' said Ang, pointing to it triumphantly. 'And sense,' he continued, pointing in the other direction towards a very neat line of carefully trimmed flowerpot-shaped bushes. The stone and lines of Montacute – grand, almost too grand though they are – give this part of the story a Gothic and mysterious flavour.

The public visit, casting curious glances and smiling shyly but making no enquiries or requests. Medieval oak-panelled rooms and very good-looking cows. I'm hungry. Hugh L. and I still regretting the frankly disastrous cream tea we scarfed yesterday.

Bad news. Big George died at 3 a.m. yesterday. Debbie is in a terrible state. She loves them so and he was a remarkable horse. Enshrined forever, I hope, as one of the most romantic quadrupeds who ever lived. Greg very upset too. We made tea and Deb told us the story – a ruptured colon. Very quick, mercifully, and totally unexpected, nothing could be done. Grave news and we try to cheer ourselves with thoughts on his film credit and flowers.

Now we set up a very complex shot on Alan entering with a very wet Kate, the Palmers and Elinor rushing to him and between them carrying Marianne off and leaving Brandon standing exhausted in the middle of the hall. Ang wants to do it all in one shot so it will develop from a two-shot on Brandon and Marianne into a single shot on Marianne into a four-shot on Charlotte, Mr Palmer, Marianne and Elinor and back into a single shot on Alan. It's going to be difficult and superb, I hope, if it works. Huge numbers of people watching and a lot of Chinese press.

Everyone very excited by this shot. It's so different to the style we've had to use in dialogue scenes where there's far less movement. Put on my costume. Barrier against the twentieth century. Funny how alien they feel at first and how safe and full of history they become surprisingly quickly.

Ang, on returning from a restaurant: 'The acting in England is much better than the food.'

Thursday 1 June

The worst news. Christopher Reeve (with whom I worked on *The Remains of the Day*) has been badly hurt in a riding accident. Black, black day.

Sense and Sensibility is about love and money. Perhaps its main question is, can love survive without money? A pithy question. Romantic codes teach us that love conquers all. Elinor disagrees. You need a decent wage, a competence. Some people need more. Some people need more money than love. Most people would rather have love with a comfortable amount of money. It's a difficult thing to accept. It cries out against all our cherished ideals. But interesting that our 'western' romantic symbols cost a great deal. Roses, diamonds . . .

The lawn is covered in daisies, which indicate the wrong season. Chris Newman asks all the members of the public who are watching to pick them off. Wonderful image as they all kneel obligingly and get to work.

Journalists on set. One informed me she'd seen *Carrington* in Cannes and didn't like it. 'Oh,' I said.

I'm so exhausted today that any extra demands make me tetchy. Must stop smoking. My one roll-up idea develops into five or six and it's madness.

Harriet Walter and James Fleet are back, commenting on the real oddness of having been away so long. I felt like that on *Remains* – missed everyone terribly and wanted to work more. It's a great privilege to be completely involved from start to finish.

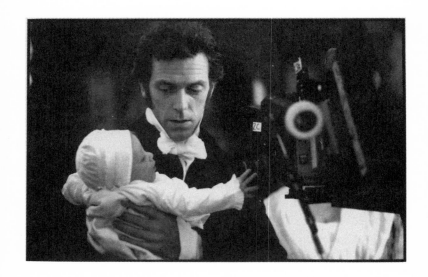

Dinner with everyone, which nearly killed me. Staggered into bed at 11.20 and woke with the light at six. Glorious light.

Friday 2 June

A bugger of a day as it's sunny and there are four huge windows, which makes lighting the room exceptionally difficult – and we've a crying-baby shot in every scene. Ang furrowed, hand against his cheek, all morning. So much to do. Much tension. Mick never wanted to shoot here because of the windows. It's supposed to be wild and stormy – what if the sun shines all day? We'll have to build platforms and create the weather outside each separate window. Impossible in the time. We were lucky. It clouded over.

Thinking up lots of additional dialogue keeps me busy. We've hired the calmest babies in the world to play the hysterical Thomas. One did finally start to cry but stopped every time Chris yelled 'Action'.

Later: Babies smiled all afternoon. Buddhist babies. They didn't cry once. We, however, were all in tears by 5 p.m. Very fractious. By 8 p.m. we were all in an antechamber telling stories to keep ourselves awake.

Saturday 3 June

Bed with a pill at eleven. Woken at three by the birds, at four by the draught and at six by the light. In to work with a stiff neck for 8 a.m. Pissing down. Perfect. Must finish early as the move to Salisbury will kill everyone. Haven't had enough sleep this week and next week is night shoots. I'll look ninety.

Imelda (*to me*): 'You'd suit a bad perm.'

Very nice lady served us drinks in hotel and was followed in by a cat. We all crooned at it. Alan to cat (*very low and meaning it*): 'Fuck off.' The nice lady didn't turn a hair. The cat looked slightly embarrassed but stayed.

Sunday 4 June

8.40 p.m. State of shock as we arrive in Southampton to ghastly modern hotel on a roundabout. After our protected, countryfied existence it's a rude awakening. I am melancholy. Tomorrow a gigantic day so am putting self to bed severely early.

Monday 5 June

6.40 a.m. Grey skies. Slept so well I'm a new man. And that's unusual. Will cloud burn off?

8 a.m. We're about to do line-up for a scene that's thirty shots, two cameras and almost the entire cast. Very seriously overstretched. One can feel everyone's sinews tautening.

9.30 a.m. Make-up and hair full of people going from pillar to post. A line-up of staggering complexity. Lots of folk from the *Much Ado* crew have joined to do Camera B. Still can't work out weather. Morag relieved to find I'd slept. I'd started to look exhausted. Must be disciplined this week.

The curtains in this new hotel are very efficient so the light didn't wake me at four. I like it here.

Ang looks rested and says there's a decent Chinese in Southampton. Phil, he and Mick very anxious about the amount we've got to do. Hugh Laurie felt the line 'Don't palm all your abuses' was possibly too rude. 'It's in the book,' I said. He didn't hit me.

Lunch. We've managed the Louma crane (from which the camera, sans operator, is suspended) shot and that's all. Didn't turn over till 11.30. Period cows with balletic horns. Excitement. Today's work will have to be completed in two weeks' time. It was always impossible to get this in a day and we can't shift the night shoots which start tomorrow, willy-nilly.

9 p.m. Just back. Think I'm allergic to horses. Did about six shots out of the thirty. Two set-ups on the Louma crane, two on Camera B and a dolly shot on Camera A which brought Nick very dramatically in on a wonderful horse, scattering period cows. Imogen had a radio mike taped inside her parasol so the angles she held it at became rather crucial. Lots of standing about. I smoked too much. We've much more to do but what we got was divine. Mrs J's hat figured largely.

Tuesday 6 June

Night shoots. 7 p.m. Wilton – the home to the Earl of Pembroke – is our location for the interiors of the ballroom sequence where Willoughby encounters Marianne and makes it clear that their relationship is over. It's a breathtaking place. Camera crew already tense about the size of the rooms and the difficulty of shooting anything in them, let alone with a crowd of extras.

9 p.m. Waiting to dress. Tension mounts. No time to rehearse. It's dark. Think I'm getting conjunctivitis. Saveloys for breakfast. A hundred extras in evening dress, every one differently characterised, from soldiers and lawyers to fops and dowagers. A monumental effort on the part of costumes, hair and make-up. Lindsay is bowled over by it. Dancers rehearse and candles are lit in rooms full of ancient and exquisite paintings. I've lost weight and my evening dress feels loose. Pulled boobs up as far as they'd go but they're still disappointing.

Midnight. Completed first shot. Liz Spriggs on fine form as the engine of the scene. The interiors are extraordinary and we're so agog there's no problem in playing the awed Misses D. up from the country.

3 a.m. Sewn back into costume after a spot of veg curry which is already playing havoc with my colon. Rather tense line-up for Robert Ferrars (Richard Lumsden) being introduced. Of course it's very sparsely written on purpose as I didn't want to lengthen script

with unnecessary introductions, but now it feels rather bald. I'm adding things, and trying not to panic.

Jane Gibson (movement teacher) is back. I stand up as straight as I can. She fixes me with a beady eye: 'Don't slump.'

We've done the antechamber and are moving into the ices room, which is full of beautiful syllabubs and sorbets made of icing sugar. A million different problems need to be addressed and everyone's point of view is necessary for the scene to work, which means shooting it from each character's angle of vision. With eight or nine characters present and not enough time to shoot everyone singly, the first problem is to work out where to put everyone so that we can include two or three people in a single shot. Then you have to avoid 'crossing the line'. This is a mysterious business. It's up to the director of photography, operator, director and continuity person to keep tabs on 'the line'. If you cross it the effect can be disastrous – people are looking in the wrong direction, essentially, so the screen grammar goes to pot. Where 'the line' is from moment to moment is sometimes so complex that I've known continuity people who've been in the business for decades to scratch their heads and take a long time to work out where the actor should look in relation to the camera.

A small knot of people gather in the middle of the room and scratch their heads. Even I've started to clamp my hand to my cheek. Ang's has been glued to his for hours. Also on night shoots each person's low point comes at a different moment so eyelids droop from 1.30 a.m. onwards at varying intervals. Smoke too. This is produced from a little canister and wafted about the room. It diffuses the light and is very effective on camera but it eats up the oxygen. Kate felt sick and then wanted to cry. She can't afford to, it takes too long to re-do the make-up. I do Jimmy Cagney impressions to distract her. She asks me to go away. My Uncle George is playing an extra in a powdered wig. Alan Rickman sent a huge quantity of chocolate to keep us all going.

Wednesday 7 June

Back to hotel by 9 a.m. Shoved a fig into my face and went to bed. Woke at 1.40 p.m. for a pee and a moan, went back to sleep till five. Quick shower and back to base for make-up. Drops from local doctor (a dish, incidentally) for incipient eye infection. Very sore. Paul the medic run off his feet. Kate's foot has swollen – inexplicably.

Immensely thrilling line-up with all the dancers and musicians. One camera on a platform and one on the dolly. Managed first dolly shot and top shot by eleven-ish. Stuart Hopps is brilliant with his choreography. He seems to be able to teach it without saying anything. The ballroom looks wonderful. Huge fire. Lights hidden in false pillars and then an incongruous collection of Mick's paper lanterns hanging from the painted ceiling to light us. Met Henry Herbert (Earl of Pembroke), a charming man who's just worked with Ismail (Merchant) and is still reeling. Tried to remember the dance steps I'd learned six weeks previously, dropped my stole and tripped up every single dancer in the set. No real food or drink allowed in these rooms on pain of death so this looks like the teetotallers' ball. I'm hoping the audience will assume eating and drinking goes on elsewhere, mainly in the ices room.

Elinor bumping into Willoughby feels good and exciting, especially coming out of the comedy between her and Robert. I had never imagined this scene occurring in so many different rooms but Ang's vision is full of movement – and notions of class. He's put Willoughby's party into yet another room – even more elite than the rest – so when Marianne sees the portrait of wealth surrounding him the message is crushingly clear. Kate probably won't get on camera tonight but is staying up anyway to remain on a similar time scale. The combination of heat, smoke and airlessness affects eyes and energy.

Thursday 8 June

Kate's got phlebitis in her leg and a limp; my eyes are pinker than Ang's breakfast buns. Home this a.m. at 7.30. The boys had a beer. Bed eightish – restless but I must have slept till four, because I had a dream about Betty Bacall. Also about laughing. One rarely dreams about laughing. Interesting. Pat Doyle's fault probably. He's the composer. Scottish. One of a family of about thirteen so the effort to get noticed in a crowd has never worn off. He makes me laugh almost more than any human being I know.

It's raining, which makes everything much more difficult and damp. Everyone gets wet travelling between base and the set, so make-up and hair are run off their feet. The dailies, Lindsay says, are fantastic.

Scrambled eggs for breakfast at 6 p.m. Don't eat much through the night. Even the extras are having a good time, they say. Ang munched illegal bread on set and giggled. He's happy, I think. Troublesome rehearsals but I hope all will be well.

Kate came down stone stairs very carefully in order to protect her leg, slipped and hurt her wrist. She's at the hospital now having an X-ray. Frankly, I'm not expecting her to survive the night.

I had a glass of water in the Earl of Pembroke's sitting room, which is the size of a field. My eyes have decided to recover a bit and nobody's cried yet so we must be doing well.

Miss Grey (Lone Vidahl) arrives. She's gorgeous. Much better-looking than any of us, and that includes Paul Kemp. Everyone stares.

Kate is back. It is just a sprain. Bandages everywhere.

Friday 9 June

Slept from 6 a.m. to 3.20 p.m. We're unexpectedly well ahead and will be able to go back for pick-ups in the ices room. Huge tax bill arrived so somehow I've got to get to a bank. Hugh L. kept treading on the train of Imelda's dress, which pulled it down so far it exposed her boobs. Keep it in, I said, but she wouldn't. Fed up with breakfasts. Caterers grey with fatigue.

Saturday 10 June

Champagne on wrap: a gift from Ang to the crew. We must've woken the Herberts up squealing. Marvellous week. James Fleet did his close-up last at 6 a.m. and made everyone laugh so much he got a round of applause. Subtle mobility of his face bewitchingly funny. I could watch him for hours.

Sunday 11 June

Drank far too much last night and woke at 5.30 a.m. Could've gone on drinking all night. Quite grateful for a hangover, it provides a bit of peace. Walked on to my balcony completely naked last night and took the couple that have moved into the suite next door slightly by surprise. Walked back in calmly affecting insouciance and then bit all my pillows, one after the other.

Monday 12 June

Back to Trafalgar to shoot interior scenes in Sir John and Mrs Jennings's drawing room at Barton Park. Lucy reveals to Elinor her engagement to Edward. Two days' work and lots of acting. Imogen a wonderful combination of coy and calculating. Kate's phlebitis much better and my eyes clear.

12.45 p.m. First shot of day. Robert Hardy extemporised a wonderful story for Margaret as they play with the map. Spontaneous applause from crew. Late finish 8.20.

Tuesday 13 June

Took a full thirty seconds to work out where I was this morning. Fried eggs and Florentines have produced a spot. Very painful morning – five and a half pages of dialogue with seven actors involves a lot of clever footwork. We all play the scene amid a welter of flags and lamp-stands trying to provide eye lines as the crew go cross-eyed trying to avoid crossing the line, which would appear, in this scene, to be in fifteen different places at once. It all goes something like this: Ang works out what he wants the actors to do. The actors keep saying, 'I wouldn't do that – I'd do this.' Specifically, I say, 'If I've just heard the man I love is engaged to someone else, I'd sink into the chair behind me, not one halfway across the room.' So things get changed, agreed to and the actors go off to make-up. Then the camera crew say, 'I can't shoot this' or 'We can't light this', and everything gets changed again. Then the actors come back and say, 'I can't do this', so it all gets changed again. We don't finish the scene. Lindsay looks for another profession. Mick swears that Ang swore when they first visited the location that there would be only two shots involving the windows. Ang has changed his mind. Mick looks for a different profession. Lindsay and I are upset about two paintings that seem very out of place in Sir John's house but which Ang is devoted to. Also we complain about the size of the room, which doesn't seem big enough to 'take a turn' in. Ang looks for a different profession. 'It's murder,' says Mick, but his cold sore is better.

Wednesday 14 June

New location: Mompesson House in Salisbury. We are using it for Mrs Jennings's London house – all exterior scenes, plus the drawing-room, bedroom, hall and breakfast-room scenes. The Lucy-meets-Edward scene has already been shot in Devon. There are only eleven people allowed in any room at one time. I understand the structure needs protection but why eleven? A volunteer stands outside counting and calls out at intervals, 'Could someone leave, please?' They're not keen on us at all.

I got four hours' sleep. Wired, after doing the difficult bit of the Lucy scene last (of course).

Base camp has been set up in the car park of Salisbury

Cathedral. Kate and I walk through the cathedral grounds to Mompesson. Hardly anyone gives our bonnets and empire lines a second glance.

Liver and bacon for lunch after three short scenes all covered in single shots in the bedroom. Good swift work.

Lovely fax from Sydney Pollack (executive producer) saying how much he's enjoying dailies. He's extraordinary – working like Hercules on his own film, *Sabrina*, but always finding time to watch our stuff and comment regularly. I'm glad he likes it. During the early stages of the scriptwriting it was he who asked the most useful questions.

'I'm from Indiana,' he said; 'if I get it, everyone gets it.' He wanted to know why Elinor and Marianne couldn't just go out and get a job. Why was Edward so dependent on his mother, why he keeps his promise to Lucy when he clearly no longer loves her. Why Elinor keeps her promise to Lucy and does not reveal the engagement even to Marianne. The probity of these people is difficult to accept sometimes – but it is balanced with behaviour of quite the opposite kind from Fanny, Lucy and Willoughby. Elinor and Edward seem both to belong to the eighteenth century, the age of Augustan reason. They are firm, balanced, judgemental, drily humorous, far more Alexander Pope than Walter Scott. Marianne shoots towards the middle of the nineteenth century, embracing each romantic ideal like a new lover. The turn of a century seems always to produce a Janus-like generation, some clinging to old systems, some welcoming the new age. Always a powerful time. As for 1995, hm. Difficult times. Everything more confused than ever for women. Haven't got the strength to think about it.

Back at Trafalgar, we're doing a carriage scene on a low-loader. This is a vehicle upon which is slung the carriage and the camera together so when it moves, the carriage seems to move. Five more scenes to do today. Kate and I are zombies, smoking, crunching peppermints and drinking water. Only achieved one take in the low-loader – it takes so long to set up. Added difficulty of finding a stretch of country road free from modern articles. Ang rode off on a bicycle and didn't return. Found him locked in the loo at Trafalgar, having broken the key. He's being rescued at present.

6.30 p.m. after tea and toast. Still waiting to do our side of the carriage shot. Ang said today, 'Only three more weeks.' I said I was planning a breakdown. He nodded and said, 'The blues – for two weeks, I think.' Most films take a week of the blues to recover from, he says; this one will take two. I was rather flattered. Seriously, though, I feel I shall never be the same again.

Thursday 15 June

Kate did her breakdown scene wonderfully well. In nearly all the weepy scenes I've tried to get one good joke. Less indulgent.

Friday 16 June

Doing Elinor's 'What do you know of my heart?' Why did I write a scene with so many words in? Endless. But Mick, Ang and Phil worked through it merrily enough and we managed not to cross the line.

I've hardly noticed Salisbury but it is exquisite. We sit like a cricket team on the green outside Mompesson. Taramasalata for breakfast. James Schamus is back. Said he rang Columbia's distribution arm and got our executive's secretary, who said, 'Sense or What?' He'd never heard of us or it.

The set infested with tapestries, little circles of women, sewing. Very eighteenth century.

Interesting and difficult scene this – getting the level of Elinor's explosion just right. The level of control. I rely entirely on Ang – I can't quite get outside it. Pleased so far and hope I can hit it again this p.m. Barely able to eat, stomach knotted. We shoot largely out of sequence, of course – so I've already done the loss of control in the last scene, which I tried to make as involuntary as possible. A case of the diaphragm taking over. I remembered going to the bank shortly after my father died to try and sort through his papers. I was feeling perfectly calm and sat in the office talking to the manager when suddenly my diaphragm lurched into action and I was unable to do anything but sob help-lessly. Walked home, shoulders heaving, thinking, This is weird, because I couldn't stop, there was no possibility of controlling it. It's never happened before or since and was as though the emotion was quite disconnected from actual thought. That was what I wanted to duplicate for the scene when Elinor finds out Edward isn't married. *This* moment, though, is much more one of anger – which I've always found very difficult. It's a hotness that's hard to simulate, a sharp heat. She's furious with Marianne but hates feeling the anger and doesn't know quite what to do with it. Like watching someone trying to bottle a genie. In the event I play it several different ways so that during the editing Ang has plenty of choices. He won't know what the right note is until he sees it in context. This is the real bugger with film – sometimes you cannot tell where to pitch an emotion and the only safe course is to offer up as many alternatives as possible.

Saturday 17 June

Hung over again. Got up this morning and could not find my glasses. Finally had to seek assistance. Kate found them inside a flower arrangement. Bags under my eyes purple.

Suddenly realised that for five years, every time I've finished a job I've gone back to rewrite this script. This will be the first time I can actually stop. Take it all in.

Weather dull and we're all a trifle confused because the scene numbers keep changing. Hugh and Greg are playing the blues on their guitars.

Raining, of course, so I am doing bastard close-ups on camera with the hangover from hell. Fine but weary and giggly. Later in my trailer, the boys are in to watch the rugby – wild with excitement and very apologetic. South Africa *v.* France. Apparently it's very important. Telly dodgy so Hugh has to hold it above his head at a 45-degree angle. They take turns to watch and yell. Tremendous business, sport, really. I wish I could get that worked up about it. Do you have to grow up with it? The boys' faces lit up with pleasure and excitement, it's really very inspiring, she said, sounding a hundred and four.

Sunday 18 June

Watched *Blind Date* and picked my feet.

Monday 19 June

Delaford picnic scene outside at Trafalgar. Ang delighted with a large pile of Melton Mowbray pork pies which he calls pork buns. A holiday atmosphere in this wonderful weather but we are really up against it. Schedule changed again today as we desperately try to cram all the remaining material into the Salisbury section. Ten weeks have gone – hard to believe I'll be home on Sunday. Finished picnic. Huzzah. Now we move indoors to do the scene where Brandon watches Marianne making a silhouette of Willoughby. Very hard to light but Willoughby's profile behind the screen is effectively erotic.

I wasn't hungry at lunchtime and am now reduced to eating leftover mince from someone's plate and fudge. People have started to talk about the wrap party. Christ. Two and a half weeks yet and a lot of big scenes so I'm in no mood for count-down. Maybe we'll have a live band . . . Chinese food? Thinks.

Tuesday 20 June

Much to do. Tension. The sun yesterday produced vicious red welts on everyone, like jellyfish stings. Most sinister, I thought. Bed with a roll-up, a beer and a sleeping pill last night. Not the happiest combination.

Did 'intolerable woman' very quickly at 9.15 a.m. and continued p.m. into Brandon's first entrance. Strain telling on me today. Pronounced around the eyes so of course we did a stills session. Ha.

The day of a thousand shots. Gemma fainted twice. Affected by fumes from the generator, we think, plus corsets, heat and airlessness. Paul had to give her fifteen minutes' oxygen the second time. Terrifying. Ang hanging in rags. I've got low blood pressure and cystitis. Excellent.

Alan was very moving. He's played Machiavellian types so effectively that it's a thrill to see him expose the extraordinary sweetness in his nature. Sad, vulnerable but weighty presence. Brandon is, I suppose, the real

hero of this piece but he has to grow on the audience as he grows on Marianne. Making the male characters effective was one of the biggest problems. In the novel, Edward and Brandon are quite shadowy and absent for long periods. We had to work hard to keep them present even when they're offscreen. Willoughby is really the only male who springs out in three dimensions (a precursor to her other charm-merchants, Frank Churchill in *Emma*, Wickham in *Pride and Prejudice* and Henry Crawford in *Mansfield Park*).

Wednesday 21 June

Fitful sleep. So many scenes, so many words. Kept waking with them all trudging about in my brain. It is, of course, very cloudy as we need sun and have no more weather cover for this location. We are trying to do the 'Mr F' dining-room scene in a single morning. Chris thinks the impossibility of it will speed things up.

Gemma a bit fragile today but better.

Bleached moustache.

Ten set-ups achieved in four hours. Lay down at lunchtime and was pronounced clinically dead by most of the ADs. Sun has come out, so we're on to the second half of the Delaford picnic scene. Triumph.

Threw Laurie Borg in swimming pool after unit still (photograph of cast and entire crew). Much satisfaction all round. Being production manager is no fun. Bed 9.30.

Woken at midnight by fucking Morris dancers outside. It's midsummer's night, and they're giving it hop on the roundabout outside the pub. I know it's a marvellous tradition and all that but it seems to lose a great deal in translation. Didn't there used to be something *Pagan* about it? Looks like something John Major designed. Damn them for waking me.

Thursday 22 June

Back in Salisbury car park with many horses, and extras for the scene outside Mrs J's house. Still can't believe what we achieved yesterday. Beauteous day on the village green, just grand. Takes ages to re-set everyone, so getting lines wrong becomes hugely bad news. A gaggle of schoolchildren come and watch. Mompesson sits there like an etching.

Noon. Finish scene with Alan.

Me: 'Oh! I've just ovulated.'

Alan (*long pause*): 'Thank you for that.'

James says it looks as if we have the carriage gridlock scene back. It's been a hostage to time and budget all the way through but it is very important to Ang. He also said that the extra energy required from everyone at present to get the scenes done just makes them better. I whirled on him. 'Don't say that!' I wailed. It makes you feel the rest of it has been under par.

Ate a lunch that consisted almost entirely of fat and had to lie down, comatose.

Very crowded today, and hundreds of spectators on

the green, who are very well-behaved and seemingly interested in watching a bunch of men in shorts carrying lamps about and laying cables. Humans are rather enchanting sometimes. I get into present-giving mode, which is worrisome. Need the filming to stop so I can go shopping . . .

Friday 23 June

Everything moving at wild pace so that we can get to the Brandon confession scene first thing tomorrow. Rather bracing and good. Tension gone. Mrs Jennings's parrot makes its first appearance. It's an English parrot, George. Vicious beak action. There's something intrinsically funny about a parrot. They have a baleful air that suggests that nothing you did could ever impress them.

I wrote a new line for Liz: 'Ah, Pooter. Still alive, I see,' which she delivered impeccably.

Ang's family is back. He looks very happy. Tide has presumably come in and stayed in. Script meeting at lunchtime on the big Brandon scene. Home soon. Ma says all my plants are dead.

We sit on the green and eat ice cream in the afternoon, watched by the curious. There's a school sports day on by the car park and a most unexpectedly rally of Morgan sports cars in the cathedral grounds. And a film crew on the green . . . English life roaming on in a very E. M. Forster fashion all about us. John Major has threatened to resign. Perhaps to devote more time to

Morris dancing? It's the first bit of news I've heard for months. Realise how entirely I have been living in this world.

8 p.m. Dye roots with Jan.

Saturday 24 June

Alarm startled me deeply. Was in a dream about mushroom soup. 9.30 a.m. and I'm still dreaming. A good calm feel and start to the day. Wonderful to have Alan, in whom one can so trust. We tried to create a space in which he can move at will, so this scene has its own life and we don't interfere too much.

The story of Brandon, Eliza and Beth is really like a penny dreadful but Alan manages to bring such a depth of pain to it — and it's shocking within this world suddenly to hear of pregnancy and early death and betrayal. Lindsay drove in with me and spoke of her worries concerning the love stories — so little time to set them up. Really the sisters' lovers spend so much time off screen — and neither is ever seen acting *like* a lover. Prevented by circumstance — so it's all implication. Very difficult balance to strike — for then one has to accept Elinor's pain about losing Edward so much later. The balance will very much lie in the editing, of course. It's frightening to think we might have *enough* of Edward and Brandon and Willoughby. At least we know that over the years we've tried everything — bringing Edward back in the middle (which didn't work as there was nothing for him to do), seeing Brandon and Willoughby fight the duel (which only seemed to subtract from the mystery), bringing Willoughby back at the end: a wonderful scene in the novel which unfortunately interfered too much with the Brandon love story. I wrote hundreds of different versions and it was in and out of the script like the hokey-cokey.

Everyone reacts variously to leaving location and going home. It's both a relief and a strain after all this time. It means the family unit is split up as everyone returns to their usual homes and routines. It is bizarre how film units become large extended families in which everyone has a role. You know whom to go to for what. Roll-ups from Sid, bread pudding from Al, a hug from Mick, wit and wisdom from Lindsay, calm from Ang, female philosophy from Morag, sound advice from Jan – and to some extent this disintegrates when people go home and resume their genuine family roles. There's a sadness to finishing on location, therefore. But of course the only reason we assume these roles is because we miss familial comfort and affection. Once home, many people become more relaxed. It's a strange balance, this life.

Lindsay appears in her maid's outfit. She's appearing as a servant in this scene. I take her through curtsying. She begs not to have to speak. We're going to make her. They're still lighting. A big master and then coverage. Trying to avoid windows. Didn't start shooting till 11.30. There'll be mutiny if we're not out by six as everyone is exhausted and there's only one day off and three different London locations on Monday. Did first bit of scene. Ang distinctly underwhelmed by me.

A very grumpy crew worked on till 8.45. Alan brilliant. Goodbye, Salisbury. Goodbye, location. Hello, London.

Sunday 25 and Monday 26 June

A weekend! At home. Not on camera on Monday and took day off. Felt guilty. Crooned over plants. Cooked a meal. Trailed round house picking things up and putting them down again. Couldn't settle to anything.

Tuesday 27 June

Greenwich. Strange to be at large in London. Traffic and spectators all over the place.

Intensely irritating day – people everywhere, Film '95 (TV show), *Premiere* magazine interview and endless personal visits which, although pleasant, are hard to fit into the scheme of things. It's alarming to discover how insular you become making a film. Strangers on set can make me feel quite savage sometimes. I don't know why – protectiveness, possibly? Personal dramas everywhere. Very hot. Coffee-shop scene with Harriet, Richard and James – they were wonderful. I rushed about correcting posture of extras, making a nuisance of myself and smelling. Hugh G. in a spot of bother up LA, apparently. Something to do with a blow job. It's all right for some, I thought.

Wednesday 28 June

Little sleep. Left early to watch line-up with Tom Wilkinson (Mr Dashwood) and Gem. The first scene of the movie, therefore vital, and I wanted to be there. Tom has watched a lot of people die and spoke of their detachment. Very true.

Day off otherwise. Saw Chris Hampton, who was testing explosions for *The Secret Agent* (his next film). He wants the biggest one (surprise).

Now we wait – they've had to remove a wall because the action takes place both in the room and in the corridor leading to it and the camera needs more space to contain it. It's good we're in studio for everyone's tired and it is of course easier to control the space and light. All in good spirits, though, and Shepperton feels busy.

Hugh G. is all over the papers – who attack with typically hypocritical glee and are enjoying themselves horribly. Have written to him.

Shepperton dressing rooms slightly ropy. Old pube-infested soap in bathroom and no towels. I've got a telephone, which is a great luxury, and a view of some cars, some corrugated iron and some scaffolding. Very London.

Me (after six hours' waiting for line-up): 'I'm off. I hate waiting when I'm not working.'

Lindsay: 'Most women wait. I just found a way to make a living out of it . . .'

Gem: 'She had very big lips, that hooker . . . Bet it was a good blow job.'

Boiling heat.

Thursday 29 June

Still boiling. Decided to have Dr Harris bleed Marianne. Adds to edge. Shepperton shimmering in the heat. Difficult to sustain this tense mood. Kate's drained by playing illness. Very great build-up to 'do not leave me alone'. I shall be very glad when it's over. Reached shot 500. According to tradition, champagne (courtesy of Lindsay) was served – at lunch, so none of us could drink it.

Felt bleak about losing Morag for the last week (she goes on, with Alan, to do *Michael Collins*). But Sallie (Jaye, make-up artiste and genuine wit) will do me and we'll laugh a lot. She says she is planning a few changes. Possibly a beard.

Very shaky today. Long wait after lunch for Colonel Brandon's 'What can I do?' scene. Nice shot but a tense affair. Long chat about the line 'Barton is but eight hours away', which made me tetchy. Ang said that logically and given the light in the shots, this would be too long a journey.

'It's been in the script for years,' I snapped, unhelpfully. 'Couldn't we have had this conversation in 1993?'

Lindsay was very calm and solved it brilliantly, I thought, with 'Barton is but a day from Cleveland'.

Consumed vast numbers of sandwiches and sweated freely.

Friday 30 June

8 a.m. already stocious in make-up. We're shooting the near-death of Marianne today. Premenstrual tension strikes me and the temperature is going to be in the mid-90s. No air conditioning in the studio. Horrible feeling of constriction in chest and unable to sit or be still. Longing for the scene to be over.

9.30 a.m. Still lighting. I pace and contemplate Elinor's rigidity and how to play this version of her loss of control. Terrifying for her. Did waking-up scene and the whispered 'Elinor' from Marianne. My stiff neck came in very useful. Dr Harris bleeding her adds about three hours to the day. Ang has got excited about the shot. Elinor carries a bowl of her sister's blood into the darkness. It will take forever to light. But it's close to midday and three set-ups left to do. Sitting cross-legged against the radiator thinking about swimming in very blue salty water. Think I must try not to cry but it might be difficult. Waiting for lighting. Like waiting for the tumbril. Or an exam. The sun outside and construction noise make me feel inexpressibly melancholy. Frightened, too.

5.15 p.m. That's the close shot over with. Interesting,

as it all came out very vulnerable and scared. A child begging. Much better, I think, than adult held-in sobs. I hope it was the right way. Very little I can do about it now. Ang says he's never seen me in such a bad mood. 'It's like trying to talk to a bear,' he said. All over now and I'm back to normal.

Saturday 1 July

Put back out. Old injury from *Me and My Girl* days. Lumbar region goes into spasm. Fuck. Fuckity fuck.

Sunday 2 July

Carriage gridlock scene. This is a scene that Ang has always wanted passionately – where we see Mrs Jennings, Lucy, Elinor and Marianne arriving at the ballroom (the interiors of which we've already shot at Wilton). He wanted to see a jam of carriages – so many that they have to alight quite far from the entrance and pick their way through the mud and horse dung to the door. Evening. Pissing down.

Tried to deal with back. Acupuncture, frozen spinach, Indocid (a muscle-relaxant) and wailing. Am falling apart. Presents from Harriet, James and Liz. It really is finishing. Rather tearful, the lot of us. Pleased it's raining – it suggests ballroom will be steaming and smell of wet wool.

For reasons known only to themselves, the caterers

did a Spanish evening – paella. This will be a wonderful shot and then it's bed with my back drugs. I smoke in an empty trailer. The papers full of Liz and Hugh in a most revolting and upsetting way. Was reading Dennis Potter's last interview with Melvyn Bragg. He said he'd like to shoot Rupert Murdoch. He can't now, but I could. In the absence of an ashtray I sit flicking my ash on to the carpet. I am a slut.

Monday 3 July

New location in Rotherhithe. Church scene. ('They always kneel.') Iced back. Slept well. Started to write farewell cards, which is making me cry. Threw minor tantrum in make-up bus, which was sans kettle, and shrieked that there was a week of major scenes to do and it's not over yet.

Hanging about waiting for the carriage mock-up to arrive (a false interior constructed on a low-loader so we can just shoot through the windows). It's stuck on Tower Bridge. Debbie Kaye said that last night's scene was the biggest done with horses and carriages in the UK for twenty years. I sit in empty trailer drinking tea, smoking, tending to back. Feel like getting in a taxi and going away for a week's lie-down. Grey cold day in the East End.

The journey through London fascinating. You forget what a vast farrago it is and how ancient. I lead, I am reminded, a sheltered life in North London – a remark I made about my mother to her face when I was seventeen. Why she didn't thump me I'll never know.

Back exercises. Hobble about geriatically and beg for sympathy. No one cares. They're making a film. Feeling very emotional. Hardly a surprise; this journey – or this bit of it, at any rate – coming to an end is unthinkable and amazing. I will carry on, of course, with Lindsay, Ang, James and Pat Doyle and all the postproduction folk. But so many leave us – Mick, Phil, the fantastic camera department. A bunch of nicer men you could not hope to find. Losing Morag already was hard. Waving goodbye to each of the actors in turn is always difficult. O Christ. Drink a lot of water. Lie down. Shut up.

We've been waiting three hours now – for two bits of wood on a trailer. Kate's on loo talking to me. She's lost her Columbia dressing gown. Yvonne (our dresser – and a fabulous rock-and-roll singer) says she knows this one's mine 'because there's a large food stain down the front'.

6.30 p.m. I've finished my bit and have gone to look at the tenements. These do not, of course, appear in the book but we're experimenting with a new point of view – Brandon's as he comes to find his missing ward. It might be interesting to see a moment's worth of the pain and misery Austen refused to dwell on. On the other hand it might destroy some kind of unity. No idea. Pat Doyle is appearing, with cold sores and a dog.

Tuesday 4 July

Shepperton. About to do my entrance shot. Sal suggested a nice blue eye shadow. I managed to talk her out of it. Very difficult scene for Gem just now, who was saintly about it. I was irritating and interfered.

Home nineish. Acupuncture.

Wednesday 5 July

Back hurts. Lots to do. Did eleven takes – the family scenes are so much more difficult to capture than the emotional stuff. Primary emotions like anger, fear and sorrow, even happiness, are a doddle in comparison with an exchange of dialogue that makes Elinor and Marianne, for instance, genuinely appear to be sisters. An ordinariness, a familiarity that is profoundly elusive. No acting, actually, is what it amounts to. Turning round, then we move on to the bedroom scene, which I pray to God we finish. I think I've written all my cards. It's worse than Christmas.

After lunch I'm in rags (my hair) and I feel I should do the rest of the day in a Southern American accent. At present confined to quarters producing prop letters with a quill for the close-up writing shots. Good not to be in a corset.

Already 5 p.m. and three shots to go. Difficult to get right – an odd mixture of teasing and serious. I'm concentrating too hard on Kate and her bits and being rather bad in my own. Mick lighting away for my close-up. I keep wandering backwards and forwards shouting, 'Ready!' Drives him mad.

Weather's turned out nice and I'm having a roll-up. Started to smoke it outside but Becca told me my nightie was see-through so I've had to come back in.

Thursday 6 July

Kate and I inadvertently drank too much so I was up at five. Wrapping bloody presents. Mother's birthday. I cut a peculiarly loud rose from front garden and shoved it through her door.

Back better. Feels less fragile. Lindsay in to say that the scene with Gemma was not lit to Mick's liking and we'll have to shoot it again. Oo-er. Kate and I in right old state doing 'Dearest Papa' – frightening and too emotional, at least for this old bag. Too much emotion slopping about anyway, never mind playing scenes about dead fathers and dying sisters. Kate was calling up some tears and I whispered, 'This will be over soon and we'll be parted.' We immediately both burst into loud sobs. Having a widdle and a roll-up to recover. Hot in that studio – good grief.

Last shot on Oliver Ford-Davies (Dr Harris) to complete deathbed sequence and then moving on to tenements which I'm not in. Phil had a go at preventing my escape. 'Oh, I think you should be there – as writer,' he said, twinkling.

'Fuck off,' I replied, elegantly.

Wrap has begun with the arrival of an amazing eighteenth-century cushion from Mr Rickman.

Friday 7 July

Last day of shoot. Driving in to Shepperton at 6.30 a.m. squashed into the back of the car with all the presents and a unicycle between my knees (it's for Bernie, who, contrary to appearances, is a wild thing). Very successful morning doing Christmas. Ang very moving – loved his tea caddy but would have been happy with a teabag. Hugged me for a long time in silence. Everyone weepy.

Sun's come out. I lie down and listen to sounds of construction. We're all down at Kempton Park Race-course now. Hot. Picnicky and fun.

Last shot for me was at 7.30 p.m. Slate 549. In the carriage. Alan's got Wimbledon on. I didn't even know it *was* Wimbledon. It's the women's final. I cast aside my sweat-soaked corset in some relief while Kate collapses on the grass. She cries. I beg for alcohol.

10.15 p.m. Off home. Finished on Take 5 of Slate 550. A shot of Alan cantering against the sunset. The camera is inside a large gyroscopic white sphere, hung off the end of a small crane attached to a truck. Quite by accident I got a place on the back of the truck and witnessed the final take of the shoot go down, followed by the sun. Then we ate hamburgers and rubbery chips and drank champagne and there was much love around.

People very moved. Lindsay and Laurie cried. I just grinned from ear to ear all evening. All within Elinor's breast was strong, silent satisfaction (it's in the book).

Sunday 9 July

Real life kicks in. Weird. Fantastic wrap party. Ang gave a Chinese banquet. We sang to him. He spoke to me for some time about the joy of his job. For everyone, it's been uniquely happy. I am in a right old state of gratitude. Now cooking Lindsay's last meal in the UK and drinking beer.

Danced all night, despite back. Hugh Laurie's band played. Laurie Borg cried again. Stayed till the end. Home four-ish.

Appendices

Dear Elinor,

Robert and I have been enjoying a splendid weekend with the Prince Regent, with whom, I declare, I feel quite at home, and who is a veritable gentleman towards we ladies. He has called me 'sumptuous' and 'frivolous' by turns all weekend, and even remarked on my famous curls – enquiring whether 'God did all' or did they require 'feminine assistance'? How we laughed!

My dear Elinor – I feel the time has come to have a little discussion about the past, but before I begin, do tell – how are your precious family? Is poor, pale Marianne happy now with the marvellously competent, mature husband? I shall never forget the pathetic lachrymosity (my! the vocabulary one acquires in 'society') of her warbling, when that wretched scoundrel left her inno-cent, trusting self for material advantage. Well – he must live with his shame. We can be grateful for that at least.

Is darling Margaret behaving herself? I do so miss her mischievous ways, and have quite forgiven her the time when she placed a beetle in my soup, and then laughed fit to burst as I was carried upstairs in a faint. How could she know how close I was to choking to death? How could she know how deeply affected I was by the experience? How could she know at that tender age that one day I might be in a position to offer her assistance financially, or an entry into polite society, and might not care to forget such behaviour? I jest – and for proof, enclose a bonnet-ribbon to prettify that sweet, homely face.

Has Mrs Jennings managed to lose weight, and has your mother gained any? If only a doctor could cut pieces off one person and transfer them to another, how content we should be! For my own part, I should like to have my face pinned into my hair to remove the creases, and restore even more girlish grace than thankfully is still in residence. Robert says I am like a pretty cottage door, with roses growing about it (my curls, you see). He is quite the poet – and outshines that melancholic drear man Cowper any day, don't you think? Enough of *moi*.

Edward looked rather forlorn when we met you in the arcade, I felt. And I see the grey hair is galloping apace. But he is a good soul, and very kind, and I am sure the life of a Rector is nourishing his spirit, if not his body. Our little Alphonse said she thought Uncle Edward 'thutch a thweetheart' (she has an adorable lisp), 'because he hath a thmile like Thuki'. Thuki (Suki) is her pet spaniel (thpaniel) and does indeed resemble Edward – including the hair on his ears, and that silly wart under his chin. Is she not clever to notice the comparison?

Dearest Elinor – I gather you pine for children, and in this area there may be problems. Fear not – you can share my five (especially little Alphonse) and, I do sincerely believe, one can glean as much joy from a pet dog or a garden. Have you tried fennel? I gather this can help fertility, although, perhaps, you are too old to reap the benefits of this particular remedy. Perhaps God will intervene – especially since Edward is in such frequent contact with him!

Oh, I must tell you – the Prince has just popped his head round the corner and invited me for a midnight drive. Should I go? If only you were here to advise me . . . I am in quite a fluster. Do I wear my fur or my velvet? I shall picture your dear self and I am sure the right choice will float across my eyes. I do feel that I have come home here. It is quite odd. Perhaps I was a royal personage in a former life. Whatever – it fits me like a glove.

Now to our discussion. I feel rather frightened – as if I were opening my heart to a governess or to an irritable seagull intent on pecking out my eyes. Not that I intend any comparison – the fault is in my imagination, which Robert says is too fanciful for my own good. No, no – if you were a bird, Elinor, you would be a lovely wise owl a-brooding on your branch – whereas I see myself as more of a Jenny Wren. As for Edward, he is a duck-billed platypus with those absurd flat feet and his honking great nose. How is his sinusitis, by the way? It seemed to preoccupy him a great deal too much for his own good; but it must be awful if one lives in damp conditions, as I fear you do.

When we first met, Elinor, I confided in you (who became like a sister to me) of my engagement to Edward, and the impossible circumstances which surrounded the liaison. Had I known your feelings for him at the time I should never have embarked on such a tactless communication. Indeed, I know you will believe me when I say that such is my nature, I should have renounced him at once had I known this would have given you the happiness you sought. I must therefore chastise you for never conveying your true emotions to me, and choosing to lie to me rather than treat me as your confidante. But I forgive you – and enclose the rather soiled handkerchief which I believe was a great source of concern when, in my innocence, I chanced to have necessity of it. It was given to me by Edward in the foolish passion of his youth which has now waned with age, along with the kerchief.

For my part, I found his brother the man I sought – and will never regret my decision to give my Edward the fate he deserved. Money has never been my concern – how can one miss what one has never known? Although I believe we are not poor, I seek simple pleasures, and look for heaven for my rewards. As for Edward's mother – I need not have feared. She loves me as the daughter she never knew, and has a great weakness for my pastries. She has a great love of wrapping presents, which I share, and many is the happy hour we spend together, wrapping and chatting like schoolgirls.

So I wish you every happiness, Elinor. And never, never feel distressed about your dishonesty towards me, nor your deception of Edward. All is forgiven and forgotten – and love repairs all damage. The worst thing that could befall either yourself or Edward would be to let an oppressed conscience dull your natural charm. Enjoy what life remains to you both, unencumbered by the patter of tiny feet.

Yours lovingly,
    Lucy

PS. Robert sends warm regards to what he humorously calls 'The Wrecktory' (referring, of course, to the tragedy of your poor orchard after the gale).

PPS. Purple is a dainty colour for a skin like yours.

The Locations

Saltram House

Standing in for the Dashwood family home Norland Park, Saltram House is located at Plympton, not far from Plymouth Hoe where memorials stand to the Pilgrim Fathers and Francis Drake. The house is filled with artwork, including portraits by Sir Joshua Reynolds. Ten of his original paintings, along with priceless works by Italian, Dutch and Flemish masters, cover the walls. Saltram House is owned by the National Trust and is open to the public.

Trafalgar House

Near Salisbury, stood in for Sir John Middleton's home, Barton Park. The festive grounds provided the location for the game of lawn bowling played by the Dashwood sisters, and the music room's spectacular murals served as the background for Colonel Brandon's first meeting with Marianne. Presently unoccupied, Trafalgar House was originally given by the government to the family of Lord Nelson.

Flete Estate

Barton Cottage is located on the vast Flete Estate at Holbeton, south Devon. The cottage, which appears modest from the front, is actually a magnificent Edwardian residence when viewed from the side, a fact the filmmakers took pains to conceal. The area is renowned for its wild life, particularly rare birds, a fact of life appreciated more by naturalists than sound recordists.

Montacute House

Doubled for the Palmers' estate at Cleveland. Near Yeovil in Somerset, Montacute was built in the late sixteenth century by Sir Edward Phelips, Speaker in the House of Commons and Master of the Rolls. Now a property of the National Trust, Montacute offers a fantastic profusion of gables, obelisks, turrets and secret pavilions.

One of the most striking features of the Montacute grounds is a strange, twisted hedge which the film-makers nicknamed the 'Brain Hedge'. Deformed long ago by a freeze, and deliberately maintained in this shape ever since, this tall, misshapen hedge offered the filmmakers the perfect background for Marianne's physical and emotional deterioration.

Wilton House

The Ball visited by the Dashwood sisters was staged at Wilton House, near Salisbury, Wiltshire, a sixteenth-century mansion largely designed by Inigo Jones. Jones's love of theatre is shown in a set of state rooms unparalleled in any other English house. A series of ante-rooms leads to the Cube room (so named for its 40′ × 40′ × 40′ proportions), followed by the even more spectacular Double Cube (40′ × 40′ × 80′), a huge room blazing with gilded swags, garlands, cornices and pediments.

The room is filled with paintings, dominated by a massive portrait by Van Dyck of the Herbert family, who still owns the property. The furniture and mirrors are by Chippendale and William Kent.

Many sovereigns, including the present Queen, have been entertained in this magnificent room, and in wartime, the Normandy invasion was planned in the Double Cube.

Mompesson House

Eighteenth-century Mompesson House, which dominates Choristers' Green in the close of Salisbury Cathedral, doubled for Mrs Jennings's sumptuous London town house. Built in 1701, Mompesson is generally regarded as a perfect complement to the gothic mastery of the cathedral, but the architect and craftsmen who created the house have never been identified. Mompesson House is now owned by the National Trust.

Mothecombe House

The magnificent Queen Anne manor house owned by farmer, forester and amateur national hunt jockey Anthony Mildmsy White, provided the setting for the drawing room of Mrs Jennings's London house. The stately room provided the backdrop for many important scenes in the film, including Edward's horrified confrontation with Lucy and Elinor.

EMMA THOMPSON won an Academy Award for Best Actress in 1992 for her portrayal of Margaret Schlegel in *Howards End* and was nominated twice in 1993 for her leading role in *The Remains of the Day* and her supporting role in *In the Name of the Father*.

Sense and Sensibility is her first screenplay.

Before graduating from Cambridge University in 1982 with a degree in English Literature, Thompson acted for three years with the Footlights at the Edinburgh Fringe; with Cambridge's first all-female revue *Woman's Hour*, which she co-wrote, co-produced and co-directed; and in her first solo show, *Short Vehicle*.

In London, Thompson starred opposite Robert Lindsay in the hit revival of *Me and My Girl*, and opposite Kenneth Branagh in John Osborne's *Look Back in Anger*, directed by Dame Judi Dench. For the Renaissance Theatre Company World Tour, she was directed by Branagh as the Fool in *King Lear*, and as Helena in *A Midsummer Night's Dream*. A BBC broadcast of the early Cambridge Footlights led to many other comedy appearances for Thompson, which culminated in *The Emma Thompson Special*. More dramatic work began with roles in the BBC six-hour mini-series *Tutti Frutti* and the seven-hour BBC series *Fortunes of War*, for which she won the BAFTA Best Actress award.

Thompson's additional film credits include *Junior, Much Ado About Nothing, Henry V, Dead Again, Peter's Friends*, and *Impromptu*. Most recently, she played the title role in Christopher Hampton's *Carrington*, which won a Special Jury Prize at the 1995 Cannes Festival.